EASY-TO-MAKE OLD-FASHIONED TOYS

Eugene F. Provenzo, Jr.
and Asterie Baker Provenzo

Illustrations by Peter A. Zorn, Jr.

DOVER PUBLICATIONS, INC.
NEW YORK

FRONTISPIECE: Early Victorian toys illustrating scientific principles.

This Dover edition, first published in 1989, is an unabridged and slightly corrected republication of the work originally published by Prentice-Hall, Inc., Englewood Cliffs, N.J., in 1979 with the title *The Historian's Toybox: Children's Toys from the Past You Can Make Yourself.*

Manufactured in the United States of America
Dover Publications, Inc., 31 East 2nd Street, Mineola, N.Y. 11501

Library of Congress Cataloging-in-Publication Data

Provenzo, Eugene F.
    [Historian's toybox]
    Easy-to-make old-fashioned toys / Eugene F. Provenzo, Jr., and Asterie Baker Provenzo ; illustrations by Peter A. Zorn, Jr.
        p.   cm.
    Reprint. Originally published: The historian's toybox. Englewood Cliffs, N.J. : Prentice-Hall, c1979.
    Includes index.
    ISBN 0-486-25958-7
    1. Toymaking—Amateurs' manuals. 2. Toys—United States—History—18th century. 3. Toys—United States—History—19th century.
    I. Provenzo, Asterie Baker. II. Title.
    [TT174.P76   1989]
    745.592—dc19   88-32120
                                                                CIP

FOR SOME OLD FRIENDS:
*Lyn, Jeff, Geoffrey, Seth,
Robert, Shep, Tonia, Erin, Nicholas,
Eleanor, Christian, and John.*

AND FOR SOME NEW FRIENDS:
*Jennifer, Yoshiko, Jackson, "Baby Baker,"
and Megan.*

CONTENTS

CONTENTS.

CONTENTS.

HELICOPTER.

HELICOPTER–PARACHUTE.

PAPER-WRESTLERS.

PEEPSHOW.

PARACHUTE.

CUP AND BALL.

BULLROARER.

AEOLIAN TOP.

JACOB'S LADDER.

x

ACKNOWLEDGMENTS

Our thanks go to our parents for their enthusiasm and interest in this project. Invaluable assistance in collecting materials for the book was provided by the librarians and staff of the Newberry Library, Chicago; the Regenstein Library, University of Chicago; the New York Public Library; the Library of Congress; Olin Library, Washington University in St. Louis; the St. Louis Public Library; Richter Library, the University of Miami; and the United States Patent Office. We would especially like to thank Mr. Noel Holobeck of St. Louis for his continuing enthusiasm and support for our research; Mr. Stephen Fuller of Miami for his technical assistance in the final preparation of this book; Ms. Marjorie Walker of Miami for providing research materials from the Victoria and Albert Museum, London; and Mr. Eric Newman, our production editor at Prentice-Hall, for the sensitivity, insight, and professionalism he has shown in preparing this book for publication.

EASY-TO-MAKE OLD-FASHIONED TOYS

INTRODUCTION

Toys play an important part in the lives of children. They are vehicles for the imagination of children, as well as tools with which to instruct them about the world in which they live. Unfortunately, too many of the toys that are available to children today do not encourage them to discover or invent things for themselves. Historically, this has not always been the case. Many of the toys that were popular during the eighteenth and nineteenth centuries required the imagination and inventiveness of the child. *Easy-to-Make Old-Fashioned Toys* is about these toys and how to make them.

Children have always made toys for themselves. In doing so, they have been provided the opportunity to penetrate and understand the physical environment in which they live. As the Swiss psychologist Jean Piaget has explained, "The essential functions of intelligence consist in understanding and inventing, in other words in building up structures by structuring reality."

Often the most exciting toys for the child are those that are based upon a scientific principle. A spinning top demonstrates the idea of centrifugal force, and a picture flip-book demonstrates the phenom-

I

enon of the persistence of vision, which makes possible motion-picture films. A number of the toys included in *Easy-to-Make Old-Fashioned Toys* will probably be familiar to the reader; others will be totally new. None of them is original to this era; instead they represent toys that were popular in Europe and America during the eighteenth and nineteenth centuries.

The toys included in the present book are intended for a wide age range. Ideally, almost all children will find toys included in the book that are both interesting to them and relatively easy to make. The simplest toys can easily be made by a six- or seven-year-old child. Many will be of interest to children who are much older. Some of the scientific toys, for example, may be of interest to adolescents and adults. Significantly, all of the toys included in the book provide the opportunity for teachers and parents to work together with children in the process of creation and invention.

All of the toys included in *Easy-to-Make Old-Fashioned Toys* can be made with simple materials found in most homes and schools. Cardboard, scissors, tape, soda straws, string, scrap wood, paper, and simple tools are all that are needed to make most of the toys. The book can be used in a number of ways, depending upon the interests of the reader. Children can simply read about the toys and their history or make them for themselves. They can choose to make only those toys that are of particular interest to them, or they can progress systematically through all of the examples included in the book. Likewise, the book may be used by teachers as a supplement to scientific or historical curricula.

Ideally, the present book will involve children in the process of creation and discovery. Not only will they be able to learn about the toys that children played with in the past, where they came from, and how they worked, but they will also be encouraged to elaborate on the principles demonstrated by the toys and possibly to create new toys that are distinctly their own.

Whether you are an adult or a child, turn the pages of this book until you find a toy that interests you. Imagine for a moment that you are a child in the past discovering the toy for the first time and embarking upon an adventure of imagination and creativity. It shouldn't take long for you to realize the rich heritage of the past and its excitement for the present.

TOOLS AND SUPPLIES.

The following is a list of suggested tools and supplies that are needed to make the toys included in *Easy-to-Make Old-Fashioned Toys*. Each toy description in the book includes a list of things needed to make that toy. Most of the tools and supplies are followed by numbers in parentheses that refer to the numbers preceding the tools and supplies described below. Illustrations and explanations are included to make your job easier in getting together all of the things that you will need to make the toys in this book.

1. SCISSORS.

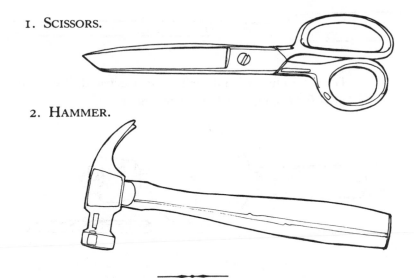

2. HAMMER.

3. PLIERS. Needle-nosed pliers should be used for bending light-weight wire; wire-cutting pliers are best for cutting all wire and bending heavier wire.

4. RULER.

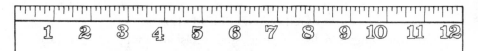

5. TRIANGULAR FILE.

6. KNIVES. Wood-cutting knife and X-Acto knife.

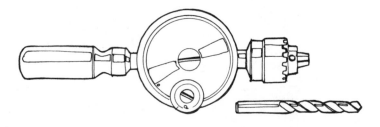

7. DRILL. Either a hand drill or an electric drill can be used for making the toys in this book.

4

8. TAPE. Scotch tape is best for holding together light-weight cardboard and paper, and masking tape is best for holding heavy cardboard together.

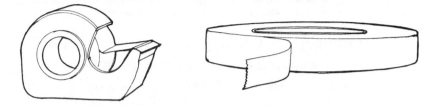

9. NEEDLES AND PINS.

10. NAILS.

11. SANDPAPER. Medium-grade and fine sandpaper are best for the toys included in this book. Both are available at hardware stores or lumber-supply stores.

12. SODA STRAWS. Flexible soda straws are used for some of the toys, whereas straight soda straws should be used for the others.

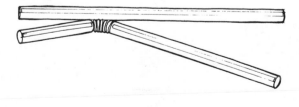

13. PENCILS. Pencils are used not only to draw and copy patterns, but also as tools to punch out holes and parts for some of the toys.

14. FELT-TIP PENS. Felt-tip pens are good for coloring cardboard and paper. Broad-tipped magic markers are good for coloring in large areas.

15. COLORED BALL-POINT PENS. Colored ball-point pens are good for drawing on clear plastic.

16. GLUE. Although many different types of glue can be used for the toys in this book, the most versatile for wood and paper is the white glue that comes in squeeze bottles.

17. FLASHLIGHT.

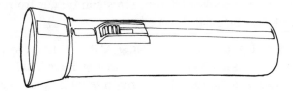

18. HEAVY WASHERS.

19. THREAD SPOOL.

20. CRAYONS.

21. THUMBTACKS.

22. TACKS.

23. PAPER FASTENERS.

24. PAPER. Plain white paper is best to use for most of the toys in this book. Different sizes can be cut from standard 8½- by 11-inch sheets.

25. SOME THREE- BY FIVE-INCH AND FIVE- BY SEVEN-INCH INDEX CARDS. If you do not have index cards around the house, three- by five-inch and five- by seven-inch cards can be cut from lightweight cardboard.

26. A THREE- BY FIVE-INCH NOTEPAD. Inexpensive three- by five-inch plain white notepads are available at stationery and five-and-dime stores.

27. COLORED CONSTRUCTION PAPER. If you don't have colored construction paper, you can fake it by coloring white paper with crayons or felt-tip pens.

28. CARDBOARD. You can get pieces of lightweight cardboard by cutting up old file folders or the backs of paper tablets. Medium-weight cardboard can be cut from gift boxes. Heavy cardboard can be cut from cardboard packing boxes.

29. MIRRORS. Rectangular and square mirrors are most useful for the toys in this book. If you can't find old mirrors around the house, inexpensive ones are available at five-and-dime and hardware stores. Some hardware stores will cut mirrors to size for you.

30. CARDBOARD TUBES. Cardboard tubes can be found on the inside of rolls of paper towels, aluminum foil, wrapping paper, and waxed paper.

31. FLAT CLOTH TAPE. Half-inch-wide hem tape, seam tape, or cotton twill will work best as flat tape. All of these are available at most fabric and five-and-dime stores.

32. WIRE. Straight wire is best for most of the toys included in this book. Medium-weight lengths of straight wire can be cut from coat hangers. Lightweight straight wire can be purchased from hardware stores and hobby shops.

33. CORKS AND CORK BALLS. Corks and cork balls are available at most hardware and five-and-dime stores.

34. STRING. Heavy- and lightweight string can be purchased at hardware and five-and-dime stores.

35. THREAD. Heavy- and lightweight thread can be purchased at fabric, hardware, and five-and-dime stores.

36. SOFT WHITE PINE, PLYWOOD, AND DOWELS. If you don't have any scrap wood around the house, soft white pine, plywood, and dowels can be purchased at lumber-supply stores.

37. CLEAR PLASTIC. Inexpensive clear plastic term-paper covers can be purchased at most stationery stores and are a good source for the clear plastic needed for toys in this book. Often this type of plastic can also be bought at art-supply stores.

A Note on Copying the Patterns Included in this Book: Many of the patterns included in this book can easily be traced over with a sheet of lightweight paper or tracing paper. If you have access to a photocopying machine, using it to copy the patterns will also work very well. In some instances the paper used for either of these methods of copying will be too light to make a particular toy. When this is the case, the tracing or photocopy should be glued onto a heavier sheet of paper or cardboard. The patterns can also be drawn free-hand directly onto the cardboard.

THAUMATROPE

THE THAUMATROPE, or "Wonder Turner," was invented in 1826 by the English physician J. A. Paris. It consists of a piece of cardboard with a picture drawn on each side and two pieces of string attached to the cardboard with which to spin it. When the Thaumatrope is rapidly spun, the pictures on either side of it merge into one.

The Thaumatrope is commonly credited with being the first cinematographic device. It provides the illusion of a single picture from two pictures because of the phenomenon of persistent vision. When an image is projected on the retina of the human eye, it remains unchanged for a period of one-tenth to one-twentieth of a second. It is this phenomenon of persistent vision that makes possible motion pictures, which are in fact single pictures showing successive motion that are run by the eye very quickly.

MAKING YOUR OWN
THAUMATROPE.

In order to make your own Thaumatrope, you will need: a piece of cardboard measuring three by three inches (28), a pencil (13) or felt-tip pen (14), scissors (1), and two pieces of string each six inches long (34).

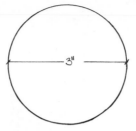

Cut a circle three inches in diameter out of the cardboard.

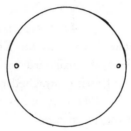

Punch two holes 180° apart from each other near the edges of the cardboard circle.

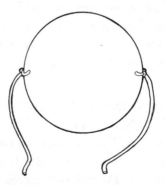

Attach a three-inch piece of string through each hole.

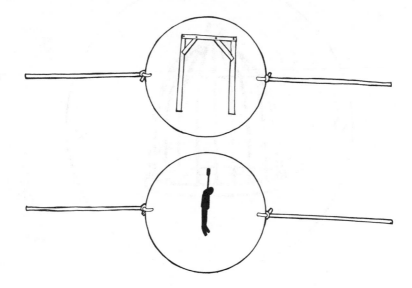

Draw separate pictures on each side of the Thaumatrope. It is important to remember to have the drawings opposite each other so that when the device is spun the two pictures merge together properly.

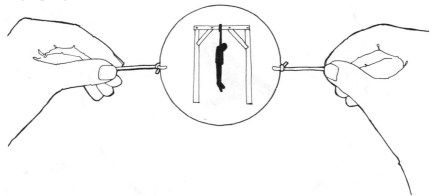

Your Thaumatrope is now complete. Hold the strings between your fingers and turn them, causing the cardboard disk to spin rapidly, merging the two pictures into one. Additional patterns for Thaumatropes are included on the following pages.

Thaumatrope Patterns.

Thaumatrope Patterns.

KITE-FERRY

KITE-FERRIES, or Kite-Yachts, were popular toys at the end of the nineteenth century. No one knows when the first Kite-Ferry was made, but they have probably existed in one form or another almost as long as men have flown kites.

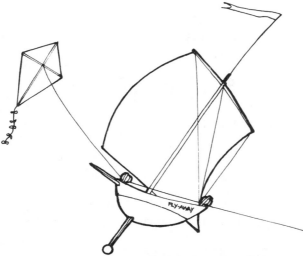

Besides being exciting toys, Kite-Ferries have been an important tool for scientists. Used to carry scientific devices, such as thermometers, barometers, and cameras, into the sky, special Kite-Ferries have been designed that will fly to the top of a kite line and return to the ground, as well as drop a parachute or glider from high in the air.

MAKING YOUR OWN
KITE-FERRY.

You can make a simple Kite-Ferry that will carry a payload as well as return to the ground automatically. In order to do so, you will need the following materials: two plastic soda straws (12), two pieces of very thin straight wire at least 16 inches in length (32), paper (24), scissors (1), tape (8), and needle-nosed pliers (3).

Cut each soda straw so that it is five inches in length. Keep the left-over pieces.

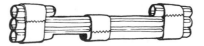

One inch from the end of one of the straws, cut a hole one inch in length like the one above.

Tape the two straws together like this (above).

Cut two pieces one inch in length from the leftover pieces of the soda straws and attach them to the taped-together straws as shown above.

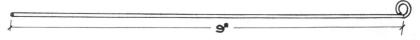

Bend one inch of a ten-inch piece of wire as illustrated above.

Insert the wire in the five-inch length of soda straw that is in the
middle. Bend the wire and insert the lower five-inch length so that
it looks like the above illustration.

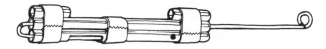

Using another piece of the wire, punch a hole in the bottom five-
inch length of straw extending exactly one-inch from the end opposite the cut-out hole.

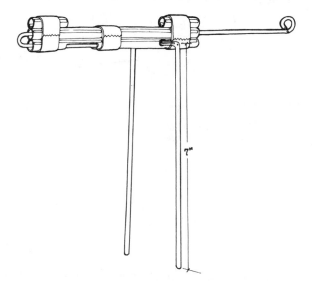

Insert another piece of wire, 16 inches in length, into the hole in
the straw. Now bend the wire at a right angle to the plane of the
hole so that there is a seven-inch length of wire on either side of the
hole.

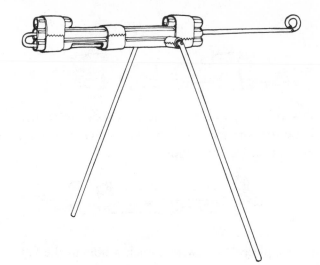

Wrap a piece of tape on both sides of the wire inserted through the straw so that it looks like the above diagram. Now spread the wires so that they can serve as the frame for a sail.

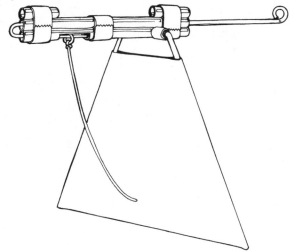

Cut a piece of paper to fit over the wire and tape it on. Punch a small hole one inch from the bottom of the paper. Put a knotted string through the hole of the sail. Attach a wire ring or loop to the loose end of the string and insert the loop through the wire-release mechanism as illustrated above.

Your Kite-Ferry is now complete and can be attached to the end of a kite string. In order to have the release mechanism work, it is important to have a "stop" placed on the kite string, as illustrated above. A large button looped through the kite string will serve this purpose very well.

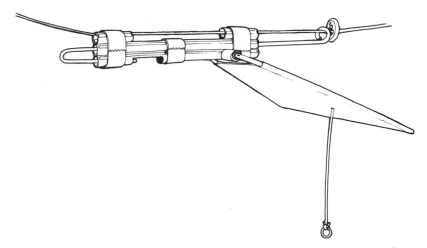

When the wire-release mechanism touches the "stop," the line holding the sail taut will be released. Once the line is released, the sail will move down the string.

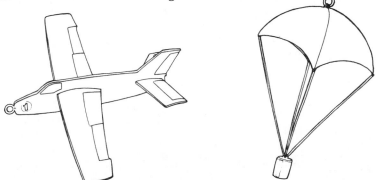

Payloads can be added to the release mechanism, such as gliders, as illustrated above, or parachutes.

PHANTASCOPE

THE PHANTASCOPE, or "Magic Disc," was invented in 1832 by a blind Belgian physicist, J. A. F. Plateau. Its discovery was simultaneous with the invention of the Stroboscope by the Austrian geologist S. von Stampfer. The two inventions are, in fact, the same device. The Phantascope is commonly recognized by historians as being the first "moving picture" machine.

The design of the Phantascope is extremely simple, it being nothing more than a cardboard circle with a series of slits equally spaced from one another around its center. A handle placed at the center of the circle acts as a pivot point around which the Phantascope can be rotated.

On the side opposite the handle, a set of sequential pictures is placed between the slits. When the device is placed in front of a mirror and viewed through the rotating slits, the pictures give the viewer the impression that they are moving.

MAKING YOUR OWN
PHANTASCOPE.

In order to make your own Phantascope, you will need: scissors (1), a pencil (13), a thumbtack (21), a piece of lightweight cardboard large enough to make a circle 4¾ inches in diameter (28), a piece of white paper (24), glue (16), and an X-Acto knife (6).

Trace the pattern shown below onto the piece of paper and cut it out.

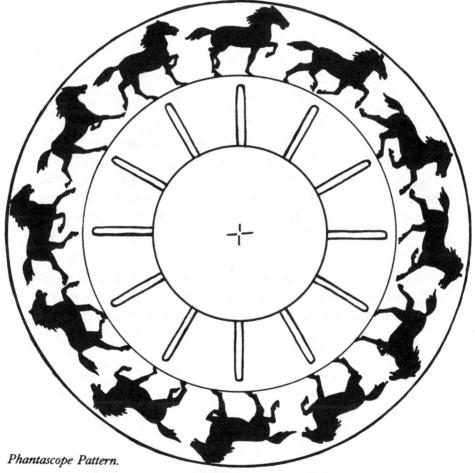

Phantascope Pattern.

Glue the pattern onto the piece of cardboard. When the glue has dried, cut out the pattern for the Phantascope.

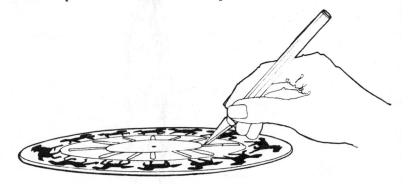

Now cut out the viewing slits in the center of the toy with an X-Acto knife.

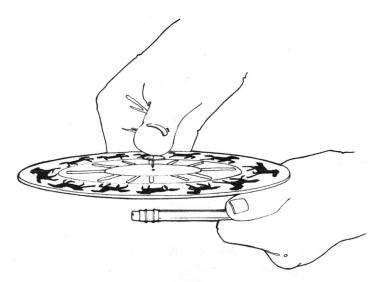

Attach the pencil handle to the Phantascope by pushing a thumb-tack through the center into the eraser of the pencil. Make sure that the pencil is on the side that is blank. Now your Phantascope is complete!

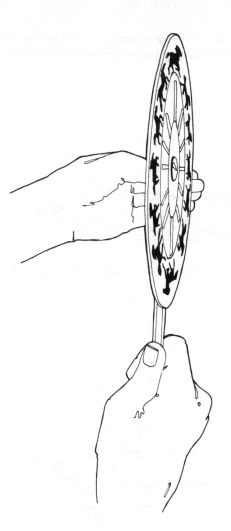

Stand in front of a mirror, holding the Phantascope so that the sequential pictures face the mirror. Twirl the edge of the Phantascope with your finger. Don't twirl too fast. Watch through the viewing slits as the images become a moving picture.

TUMBLING
ACROBAT

THE TUMBLING ACROBAT is one of many toys that employ the force of gravity in order to move. However, it is by far the most fun and the most simple.

The Tumbling Acrobat was a popular toy in China, and during the nineteenth century it was introduced into Austria and Germany, where it became a popular folk toy. The idea behind the Tumbling Acrobat is extremely simple. A ball bearing or drop of mercury was put into a cardboard or papier-mâché tube with rounded ends. When the tube was placed on a slightly inclined surface, the ball bearing or mercury would roll to its bottom. When it reached the bottom of the tube, the momentum would carry the lighter end of the tube forward. The ball bearing or mercury would then roll forward again. The toy would continue to turn over and over again until it reached the bottom of the incline.

MAKING YOUR OWN
TUMBLING ACROBAT.

You can make your own Tumbling Acrobat by using the following materials: two marbles, a five- by seven-inch index card (25), tape (8), a felt-tip pen (14), and scissors (1).

Copy the pattern shown below onto the index card, and cut the
pattern out of the index card.

Tumbling-Acrobat Pattern.

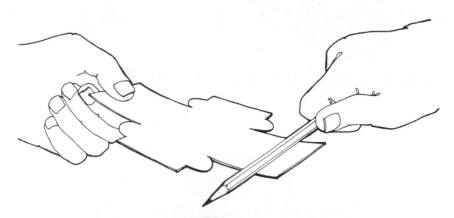

Press the cut-out pattern against a hard, flat surface, such as a table top, with the pencil or pen. Pull the pattern forward. Continue to do this until the pattern is very flexible.

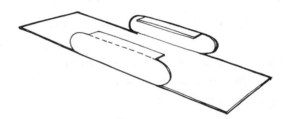

Fold the flaps on the pattern along the dotted lines.

Now tape the ends of the pattern together on the inside so that a loop is formed by the index card.

Tape one of the flaps to the inside of the loop.

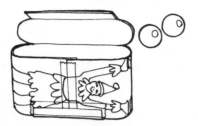

Place the marbles inside the loop and tape the other flap closed.

Your Tumbling Acrobat is complete. All you will need now is an inclined surface on which to test him out!

A tilted book will generally work as an inclined surface. If your acrobat slides down the inclined surface, it probably means that the surface is too smooth. You may need to use something that is rougher, such as a piece of cloth taped to the book cover. A piece of felt glued to a piece of cardboard will work best.

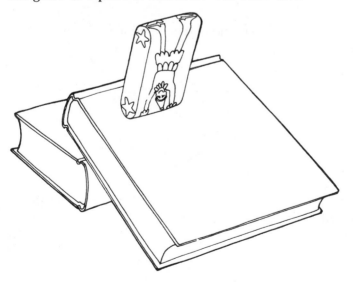

MARBLE MAZE

MARBLE MAZES are based on labyrinths, which have been popular since ancient times. In Greek mythology, a labyrinth played an important part in the legend of Theseus, who had to escape from a giant labyrinth after slaying a monster called the Minotaur. Illustrations of labyrinths can also be found on the backs of some ancient Greek coins.

Labyrinth Puzzles from Greek Coins.

During the Middle Ages, labyrinth designs were occasionally included as decorations on the floors and walls of churches and cathedrals. Garden labyrinths or mazes were also created during the Middle Ages and the Renaissance by growing hedges and shrubs in intricate patterns. These labyrinths could be solved by walking through them, trying to find the exit once one had entered them.

Mazes were adapted as toys for children in a number of different ways during the nineteenth century. Probably the most common mazes were those that were solved by tracing a path through them with a pencil. These puzzles were regularly found in children's magazines and books. Numerous games were also based on mazes. The Medieval game of Nine Men's Morris, for example, used a type of maze for its board, and the modern children's game of Hopscotch is probably patterned after earlier maze-type games.

An interesting application of the principle of the maze to a toy was the Marble Maze, or "Nerve Tester," which was introduced in America during the late 1880s. The idea of the Marble Maze was to guide a marble through a hand-held wooden maze. Holes were set throughout the maze for the marble to fall through. Scores were determined by how far children were able to guide their marble through the maze without having it fall off the edge or through a hole.

MAKING YOUR OWN
MARBLE MAZE.

In order to make your own Marble Maze, you will need: a marble, a piece of medium-weight cardboard 8½ by 11 inches (28), colored felt-tip pens (14), scissors (1), and an X-Acto knife (6).

Copy the pattern on the following page onto the piece of cardboard.

Cut out the pattern with the scissors. It will be easier to cut out the shaded areas of the pattern with the X-Acto knife. You can decorate your Marble Maze with the colored pens.

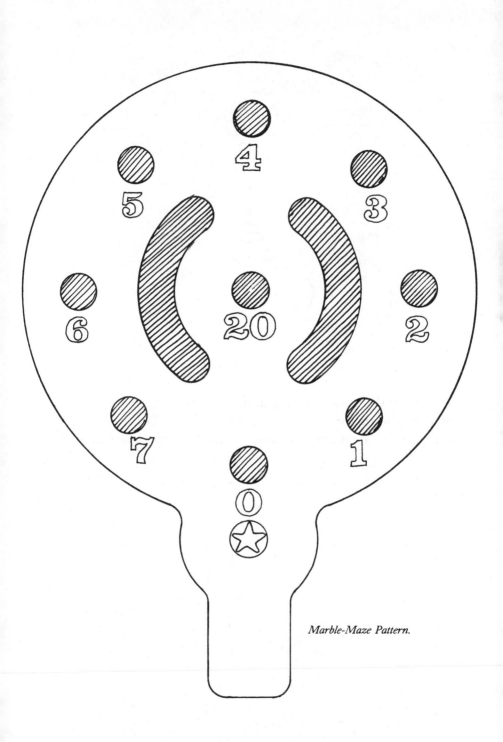

Marble-Maze Pattern.

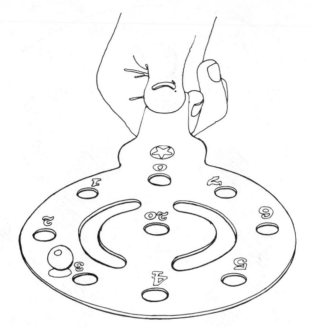

Now place the marble in the starred circle and see if you can make your way to the final hole with the highest number. If you wish, design your own mazes and make them as complicated as you want.

TALEIDOSCOPE
& KALEIDOSCOPE

THE KALEIDOSCOPE is perhaps the most well known of all optical toys. Known to the ancient Greeks, the Kaleidoscope was rediscovered and patented in 1817 by the Scottish scientist Sir David Brewster. The name "Kaleidoscope" is a combination of three Greek words that mean "an instrument with which we can see things of beautiful form." After the publication in 1819 of Brewster's *Treatise on the Kaleidoscope*, it was only a short while before the Kaleidoscope became an extremely popular toy.

In its simplest form, the Kaleidoscope is actually a Taleidoscope or mirrored Kaleidoscope. In a Taleidoscope, three mirrors are taped together. The mirrors form a hollow triangle and are placed in a long tube. One end of the tube is open and the other end is covered with a hole in its center. By looking through the hole at the end of the tube and rotating it, you could see beautiful changing patterns of whatever object you pointed at with the Taleidoscope.

In a Kaleidoscope, loose fragments of colored glass or paper were placed over the end of the tube and held in place with a paper cover. By looking through the hole and rotating the tube, you could see an infinite number of colorful changing symmetrical patterns.

MAKING YOUR OWN TALEIDOSCOPE
AND KALEIDOSCOPE.

In order to make your own Taleidoscope and Kaleidoscope, you will need: a potato-chip or tennis-ball can, masking tape (8), scissors (1), a nail (10), a hammer (2), a small clear plastic bag (37), a piece of white paper (24), facial tissues, and colored construction paper (27). You will also need three mirrors, each two inches wide and eight inches long (29).

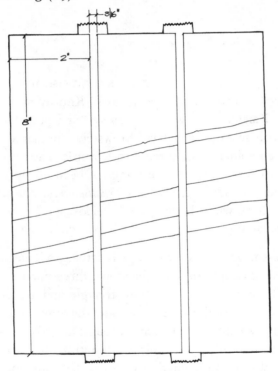

Place the three mirrors on two pieces of masking tape as shown above. Be sure to leave about three-sixteenths of an inch between the edges of the mirrors so that when you bend them together, their edges will meet. The reflecting surfaces of all the mirrors should be facing in.

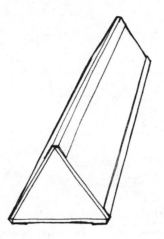

Fold two mirrors up to form a triangle as shown above. Tape the top edges together.

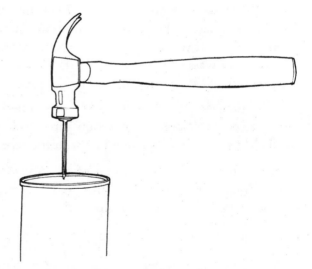

With the hammer and nail, punch a hole in the middle of the metal bottom of the can. If the hole is not quite large enough to see through, move the nail around with your hand to make it larger.

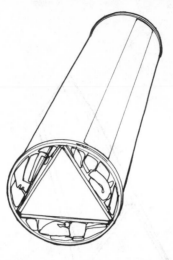

Lift off the plastic lid of the can and place the mirrors inside. Fill in the spaces between the outside of the mirrors and the inside of the can with bunched-up tissue to keep the mirrors from shifting around.

Your Taleidoscope is now complete. Look through the hole at a friend or at different things in the room and you will see many different patterns. If you want, you can experiment further by placing a magnifying glass over the front of the Taleidoscope and seeing even more interesting patterns.

In order to make your Kaleidoscope, you will need to cut many little pieces of the colored construction paper and put them into the small clear plastic bag. Seal the bag with the tape.

Place the bag over the open end of the Kaleidoscope, as shown below. Make sure that all of the colored pieces of paper are bunched together over the opening.

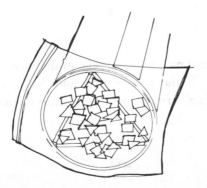

Now cut out a piece of white paper, a little larger than the bag, and place it over the bag. Bend the edges of the paper down tightly around the can.

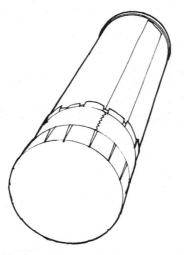

Put a strip of masking tape around the can to fasten the paper and bag tightly across the top of the can. You have changed your Taleidoscope into a Kaleidoscope.

When you rotate the Kaleidoscope and look through the hole, you can see an infinite number of changing colorful symmetrical patterns.

BOOMERANG

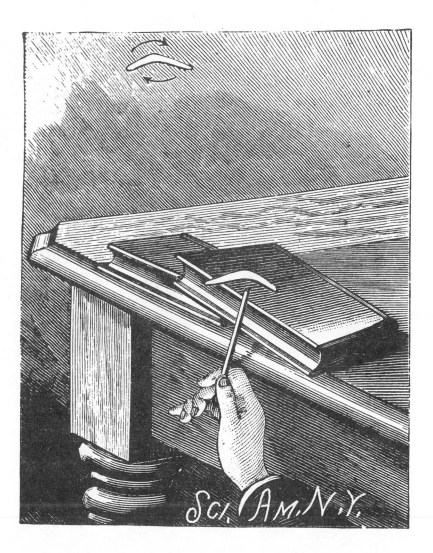

THE BOOMERANG is one of the most ancient of all inventions. In its simplest form as a "throwing stick," the Boomerang has been used by the Egyptians and various American Indian tribes, as well as by different people in India and Polynesia.

The type of Boomerang that is most well known is the returning boomerang invented by the Australian Aborigines. When thrown correctly, this Boomerang will fly through the air in an arc and return to its thrower. Thousands of years old, the returning boomerang was introduced into Europe during the second half of the eighteenth century by the English explorer James Cook.

Throwing a Boomerang.

Although the Boomerang was originally of interest to scientists who were concerned with understanding the aerodynamic principles that caused it to return in its flight, it also became a popular toy for children during the Victorian era.

HOW TO MAKE YOUR OWN
BOOMERANG.

In order to make your own Boomerang, you will need: scissors (1), a pencil (13), and a piece of lightweight or heavy cardboard (28).

Your Boomerang can be as small as 2½ inches across or as large as 12 inches. A small Boomerang can be launched off a book inside the house, but a large Boomerang (from six to 12 inches) must be thrown outdoors.

Using the pattern below, trace the shape of the Boomerang onto the cardboard, making sure that it is a true right-angled shape. Cut it out, being sure to round off the ends of the arms.

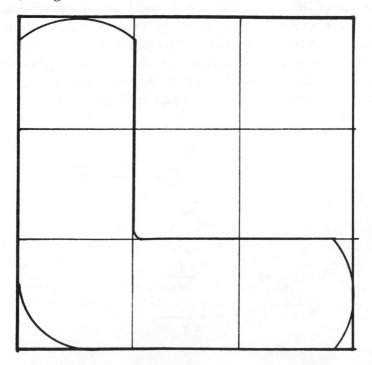

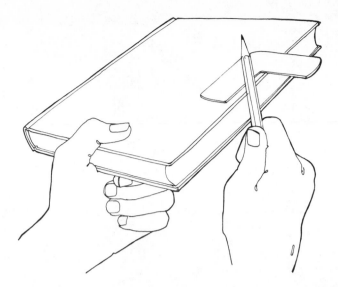

In order to launch a small Boomerang, balance it on the edge of a book with one of its arms overlapping the edge as shown above. Hit the arm that is extending over the edge of the book sharply with your index finger or a pencil. The Boomerang will fly up and away in an arc and will return to you!

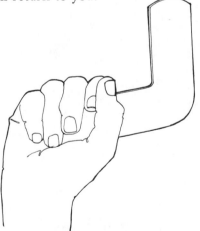

If you have made a larger Boomerang, which must be used outdoors, you should hold it between your thumb and forefinger in order to launch it. Throw the Boomerang slightly at an angle into the air and watch it return to you.

PEA-SHOOTER

PEA-SHOOTERS, often made by children during the nineteenth century, were also sold as inexpensive toys during that time. Basically, the Pea-Shooter is nothing more than a blowpipe or tube through which a projectile, such as a bean or pea, is propelled by a puff of air blown from the mouth. More complex blowguns, based upon the same principle, have been used as weapons by natives in South America, Africa, and Asia.

Most Pea-Shooters were made of a hollowed-out piece of wood or a copper tube. Dried peas, beans, or wads of paper provided the ammunition.

MAKING YOUR OWN
PEA-SHOOTER.

In order to make your own Pea-Shooter, you will need: a piece of 8½- by 11-inch paper (24), tape (8), and dried peas, beans, or small wads of paper.

Roll the piece of paper lengthwise into a tube approximately one-half-inch in diameter.

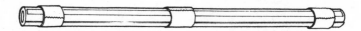

Now tape the tube together at its middle and ends.

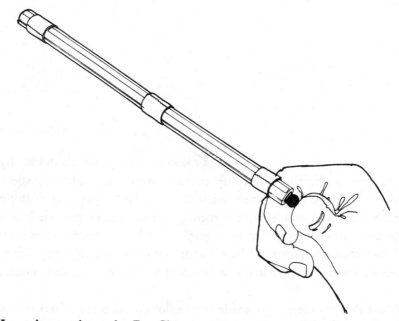

In order to shoot the Pea-Shooter, put a pea or wad of paper into one end and put your lips to the tube at the same end.

Blow on the tube as hard as you can. Choose a safe target, such as a tree or the side of a wall, to practice your Pea-Shooter on.

Never point or shoot a Pea-Shooter at a person, an animal, or something that might break.

THREE-WAY PICTURE

THE THREE-WAY PICTURE, or corrugated picture, was a special type of picture, used as a wall decoration, that was popular during the nineteenth century. Instructions on how to make Three-Way Pictures were included in numerous toy and game books from the period. The principle behind the Three-Way Picture was that it would become a different picture when viewed from the right, the center, and the left.

MAKING YOUR OWN
THREE-WAY PICTURE.

In order to make your own Three-Way Picture, you will need: three magazine pictures that are cut to exactly the same size, a sheet of white paper (24) that is equal to the width of the pictures and as long as the three when placed end to end (if you are using very large pictures, you may want to tape sheets of paper together), scissors (1), glue (16), a ruler (4), and a pencil (13).

Measure the length and width of all three pictures. Cut out a strip of paper as wide as the pictures and as long as all three pictures, end to end, as shown below.

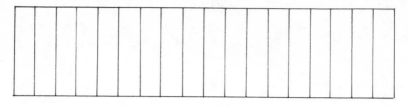

Divide the piece of paper into half-inch strips, marking off each with the pencil and ruler.

Fold the strip of paper along these lines so that it looks like the pattern above.

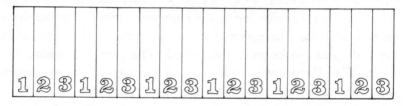

Cut a half-inch strip off one of the pictures. Glue it to one end of the piece of paper. Cut another strip off the picture and glue it onto the paper, leaving two blank strips between.

Continue cutting half-inch strips of the picture and gluing them onto the paper until you have finished one picture. Cut the other pictures into half-inch strips and glue them onto the paper in order where the sections marked 2 and 3 are shown in the illustration.

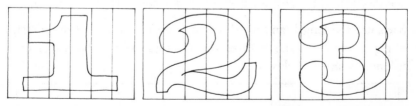

After you have glued on all the strips, you will have a confused picture that is as long as the three original pictures together and of the same width. Fold the paper up like an accordion or fan, with every third strip remaining flat while the others are pushed together.

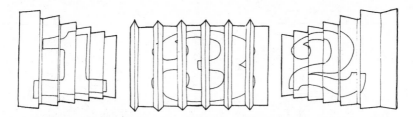

As you view the Three-Way Picture from one side, you will see one picture, but when you step in front of it and then move to the other side, you will see the other two pictures!

CHROMATROPE TOYS

T. J. W. ROBERTSON.

Toy-Chromatropes.

No. 165,123.   Patented June 29, 1875.

Fig 1.

Fig.2.

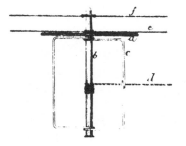

Fig.3.

Fig.4.

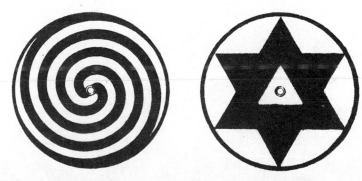

CHROMATROPE TOYS comprise many different toys, including the Eidotrope, the Toy-Chromatrope, the Kaleidoscopic Color Top, and the Philosophical Whizgig. All of these toys demonstrate the scientific phenomenon known as Persistence of Vision, the same principle that creates the illusion of a single picture when you spin the Thaumatrope.

One of the simplest Chromatrope Toys was made by threading a string through two holes in a colored disk. By pulling and relaxing the string, optical effects were produced. Similar optical effects can also be made with a rapidly spinning top of different colors or patterns. The movement of the spinning top causes the eye to combine the separate colors and patterns inscribed on it.

MAKING YOUR OWN
CHROMATROPE TOYS.

In order to make your own Chromatrope Toys, you will need: cardboard (28), scissors (1), a pencil (13), crayons (20) or felt-tip pens (14), and thin string (34).

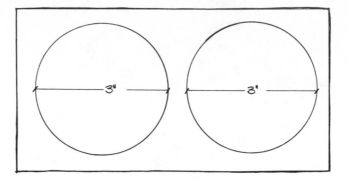

Draw two circles on the piece of cardboard, each about three inches across. You can use the bottom of a glass or a jar to draw the circles, or you can trace the patterns included with the description of this toy. Once you have the patterns on the cardboard, cut them out.

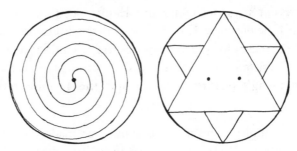

On the two circles you have just cut out, draw one of the designs from the patterns that are shown on the next page.

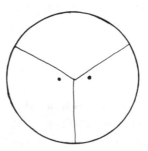

On the back of one of the circles, draw the third pattern and color all the designs.

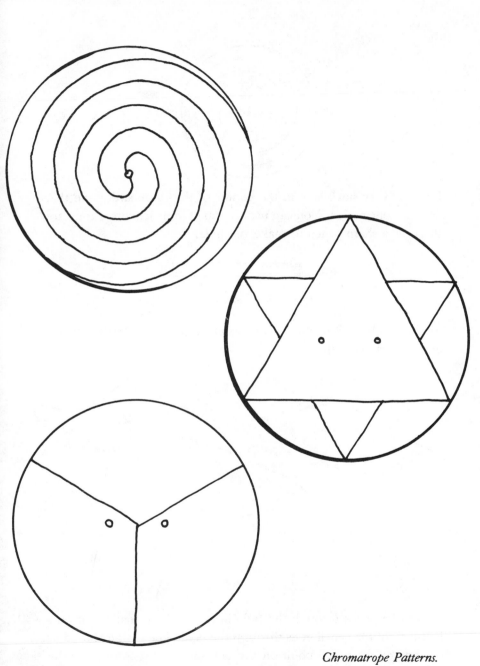

Chromatrope Patterns.
(slightly reduced)

Punch a very small hole in the center of the cardboard circle that only has one design. You can use the tip of your scissors if they are sharp or a sharp pencil to make the hole.

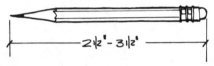

Find a small pencil, 2½ to 3½ inches in length. Or, sharpen a pencil until it is this length.

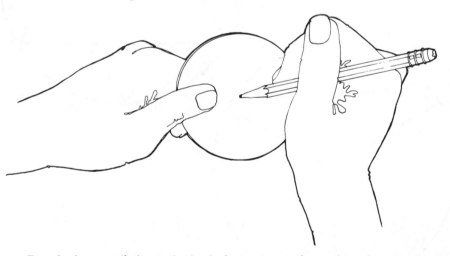

Punch the pencil through the hole in the circle so that about one-half-inch of the pencil goes through the hole. The design should be on top and the pencil point on the bottom.

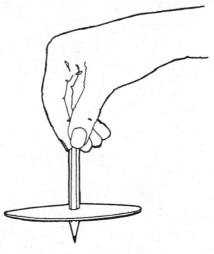

Now you have a simple top that you can spin with one hand and have the patterns change before your eyes.

To make another Chromatrope Toy, punch two holes, three-quarter-inches apart from the center of the circle of cardboard that has a design on both sides. These holes are marked on the pattern included with the directions for this toy.

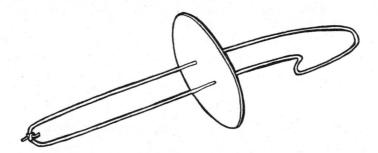

Thread a piece of strong but light string about 40 inches long through the two holes as shown above. Tie the ends together in a knot.

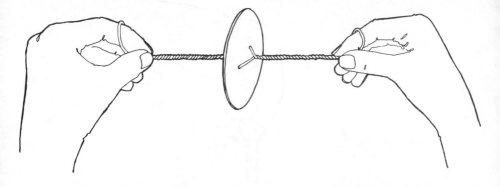

Wind up the toy by swinging it over and over in the middle of the loops with your hands, holding the ends of the string with your fingers. Make sure that both sides of the string are balanced with each other and that the Chromatrope Toy remains perpendicular to the floor, or it will not work properly. When you pull your hands apart, the circle will spin back and rewind itself. As it does this, you will catch glimpses of the Chromatrope Toy changing colors and patterns.

You can make as many circle discs and designs for your Chromatrope Toys as you like. Try different colors and designs and see how each of them works.

JUMPING JACK

THE JUMPING JACK is an animated puppet toy whose arms and legs move up and down when a string connected to them is pulled from below. Toys based on similar principles were used in ancient Egypt. During the eighteenth century, Jumping Jacks were made in France and were known as "Pantins." Often, famous artists designed these toys, and members of the French court competed with one another to see who could put together the largest collection. Made from cardboard, "Pantins" were imported into America and were popular toys among both children and adults.

HOW TO MAKE YOUR OWN
JUMPING JACK.

In order to make your own Jumping Jack, you will need: a piece of heavy cardboard 8½ by 11 inches (28), six brass paper fasteners (23), a piece of strong but thin string (34), scissors (1), colored felt-tip pens (14), and a pencil (13).

Copy the patterns (on the following page) for the different parts of the Jumping Jack onto the cardboard and cut them out.

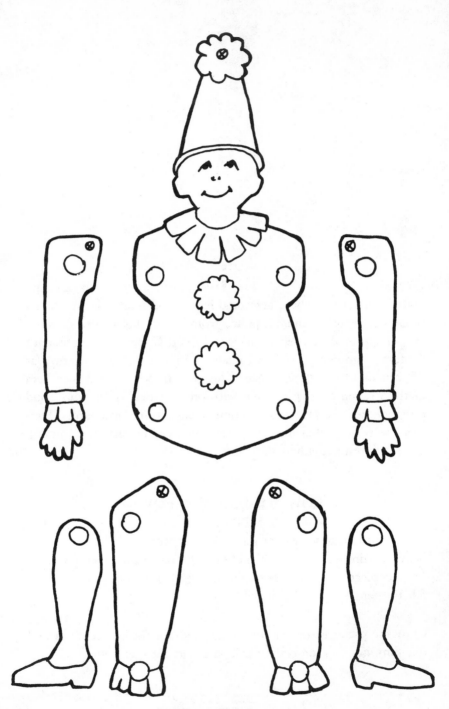

Jumping-Jack Pattern.

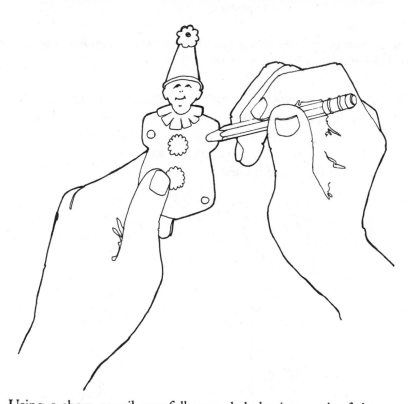

Using a sharp pencil, carefully punch holes into each of the specially marked points on the patterns. The points marked with an *x* are the places to which strings are to be attached; the points marked by a small circle are those where the paper fasteners should be pushed through the cardboard.

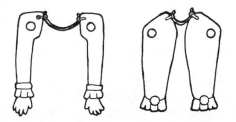

String the arms and legs by threading a length of string through the holes in the arms and the legs marked with an *x*, as illustrated at the bottom of page 81. Knot the ends of each string, making sure that the strings are not too tight.

Push the paper fasteners through the holes marked on the front side of the Jumping Jack's body to connect his arms and legs to his body. Close the prongs of the fasteners on the back side of the body. Make sure that the fasteners are loose enough so that the arms and legs can move up and down smoothly.

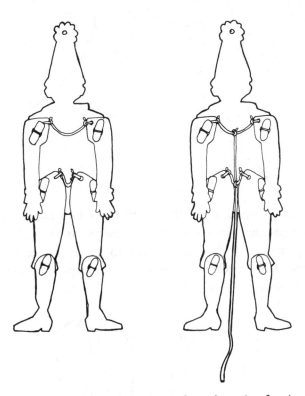

Connect the arms and legs by tying a long length of string first to the center of the string for the arms, then to the center of the string tied to the legs.

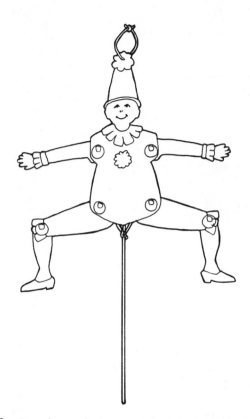

Tie a loop of string through the *x* marked in the Jumping Jack's hat and tie a knot in it. Hook this loop into a doorknob and pull on the string. Watch your Jumping Jack jump up and down as you pull and release the string.

FLOATING BALL

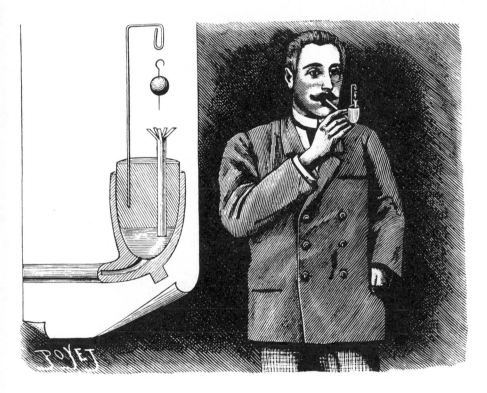

THE FLOATING BALL was one of various types of inexpensive penny toys from the nineteenth century involving the suspension of a cork ball or dried pea on a stream of air blown through a clay pipe or metal tube. One of these toys included a cork ball with a hook running through it. When the ball was blown into the air, an attempt was made to hook the ball onto a looped hook attached to the pipe. You can make a very simple Floating Ball toy with materials found around the house.

HOW TO MAKE YOUR OWN
FLOATING BALL.

In order to make a Floating Ball, you will need: a flexible plastic soda straw (12), 3¾ to 4 inches of thin wire (32), some dried peas or a small cork ball no more than three-eighths of an inch in diameter (33), scissors (1), pliers (3), a ruler (4), and tape (8).

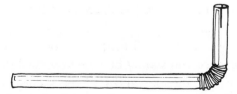

Carefully cut the end of the soda straw closest to the flexible joint so that there are four small fingers or pieces of plastic, three-eighths of an inch long, sticking out at its edge as illustrated at the bottom of page 87. Gently bend these pieces down to make a cradle for the cork ball or pea.

Be sure that the short end of the straw is bent so that it is at a right angle to the longer piece.

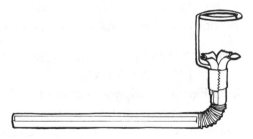

With the pliers, bend the piece of wire into the shape illustrated above.

Tape the wire loop to the top of the soda straw so that the loop is approximately one inch above the opening of the straw.

Now place the pea or cork ball on the top of the straw and blow gently. With practice you should be able to control the ball so that it will rise up through the loop and settle back down again into the cradle at the top of the straw.

FLIP-BOOK

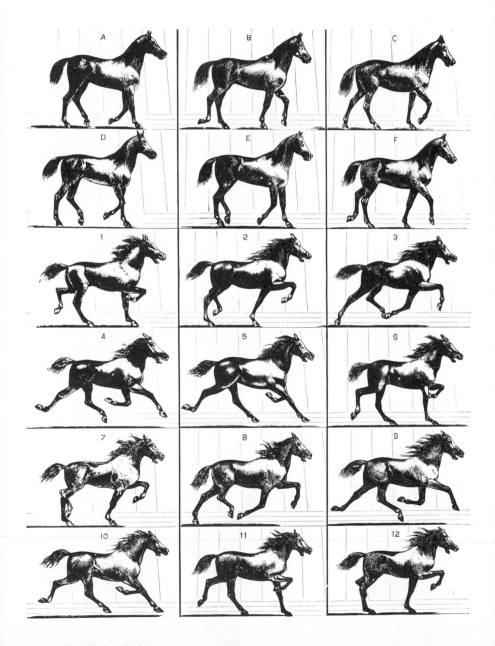

FLIP-BOOKS, or Flicker Books, were probably used by children long before they were first patented in 1868. Basically, the toy consisted of a series of sequential pictures or photographs put on separate pieces of paper, one after the other. When the book was quickly flipped through, the pictures would provide the illusion of a moving picture. During the latter part of the nineteenth century, the Filoscope, a simple version of this toy, was commercially available. The Mutoscope, which was popular during the same period, was also based upon the same principles as the Flip-Book. It consisted of a set of sequential photographs mounted on a wheel and set in a lighted box with a viewing hole. When the wheel was rotated by turning a handle mounted on its side, the viewer was provided with what appeared to be a moving picture.

MAKING YOUR OWN
FLIP-BOOK.

In order to make your own Flip-Book, you will need: a felt-tip pen (14) and an inexpensive plain white notepad, approximately three inches by five inches (26).

Decide upon a simple subject showing something moving, such as the moving hands of a clock, a bouncing ball, or a running stickman. You could also use the running horse shown on page 89. Copy each picture in order on a separate page of the notepad.

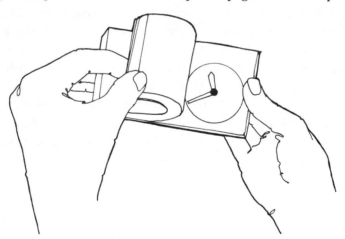

When you have finished drawing the pictures, flip through them quickly. If you have drawn the pictures carefully, they should appear to move when you flip them. By experimenting with different subjects, you can make as many different Flip-Book movies as you like.

BUZZ SAW

THE BUZZ SAW is a noise toy that has been used for hundreds of years by the Eskimos, as well as by South American Indians, who called the toy a "mou mou." By the nineteenth century the Buzz Saw had become a popular toy in both Europe and America. It was usually made out of a disk of tin with notches along its edge. Two holes were placed in the center of the disk through which a string was threaded and twisted. The disk was wound up on the string by flipping it and then rotated by pulling it in and out on the looped ends of the string. Once the disk was set spinning rapidly, its teeth were brought into contact with the edge of a piece of paper. As the teeth on the edge of the Buzz Saw touched the paper, a shrill buzzing sound was made. The speed of the rotating disk determined the pitch of the buzzing sound. When every other tooth for the toy was bent, the buzzing sound was increased.

MAKING YOUR OWN
BUZZ SAW.

In order to make your own Buzz Saw, you will need: cardboard (28), scissors (1), a pencil (13), crayons (20) or felt-tip pens (14), and approximately 40 inches of thin but strong string (34).

Draw a circle with teeth approximately three inches in diameter on the piece of cardboard. You can use the bottom of a glass or a jar to make the circle, or you can trace the pattern below.

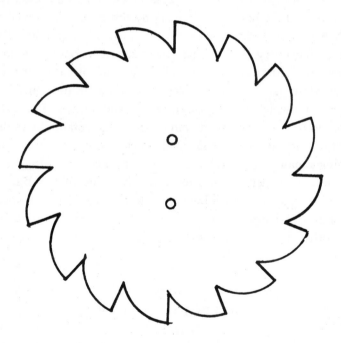

Buzz-Saw Pattern.

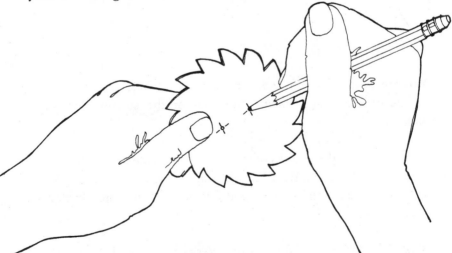

Once you have drawn the circle or the pattern on the cardboard, cut it out. Be sure to cut out the teeth along the edge of the disc as shown in the pattern. If you wish, you may use the designs for the Chromatrope Toys to decorate your Buzz Saw, or you can make up your own designs.

Now punch two holes approximately one-half-inch apart at the same distance from the center of the disk. You can use the tip of your scissors, if they are sharp, or a sharp pencil to make the holes.

Thread the piece of string through the two holes as shown above. Tie the ends together in a knot.

You can wind up the Buzz Saw by swinging it over and over in the middle of the loops, holding the ends of the strings with your fingers.

Make sure that the lengths of string on either side of the Buzz Saw are equal and that the Buzz Saw remains perpendicular to the floor. When you pull your hands in and out, the disc will spin back and rewind itself.

Now place a piece of stiff paper on a desk or table so that it overlaps the edge by several inches. Hold it in place with a book or other heavy object. As the Buzz Saw spins, bring its teeth into contact with the paper. The tops of the teeth hitting the paper will create a shrill *Buzzzzz!*

PANDEAN PIPES

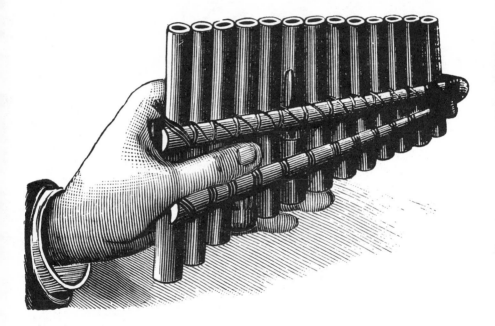

PANDEAN PIPES were described in ancient Greek Mythology as a flute-like instrument, the invention of Pan, the god of the woods and fields. Also named Pan's Pipes, the instrument has been played by both children and adults throughout the world for thousands of years. By the nineteenth century, Pandean Pipes had become one of the most popular of all musical toys.

Known also as a syrinx, Pandean Pipes have been made of such various materials as cane, wood, and pottery. Consisting of four to twelve hollow pipes, the instrument was usually closed at the bottom. The pipes were played by blowing air across the open ends at the top. They could be tuned by adjusting the corks that were often used to stop their lower ends. Half-tones could be made by tilting the pipes toward the lips.

MAKING YOUR OWN
PANDEAN PIPES.

In order to make your own Pandean Pipes, you will need six soda straws (12), tape (8), a ruler (4), scissors (1), and a pencil (13).

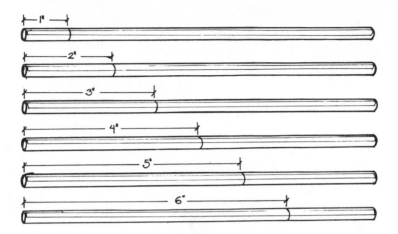

With the ruler and pencil, measure and mark each soda straw as shown above, so that the first has a mark one inch from its end; the second, two inches from the end; the third, three inches from the end; and so on until six of the straws are marked. Next, cut each straw at these marks.

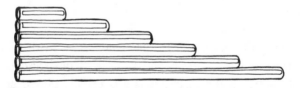

Arrange the straws in order of size from large to small on a flat surface as shown above.

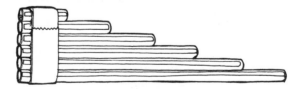

Put a piece of tape across the straws to hold them in place. Make sure that the uncut ends are precisely even.

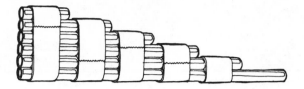

Continue to wrap the tape all around the straws to hold them firmly together.

Now you are ready to play your Pandean Pipes. Blow gently across the top of one of the straws to make a crisp, clear sound. If you tilt the pipes toward your lips, the same note blown from one of the pipes will change by a half-tone. You can also change the different notes produced through the pipes by stopping up the lower ends with your fingertips.

BALANCING MAN

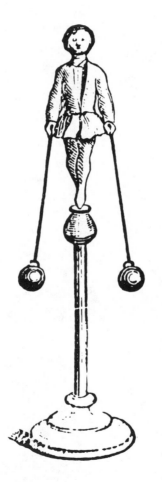

THE BALANCING MAN, a toy consisting of a circus figure balancing on a specially made wooden base, is the most popular nineteenth-century example of the many balancing toys that date back to ancient China and India. Ancient balancing toys were carved from soft wood, whereas more-modern examples of the toy used counterweights attached to them with wires. Illustrations of balancing toys can be found in magic books from the eighteenth century. Popular nineteenth-century examples of the toy included a Dancing Lady, who made pirouettes while balanced on a single foot, and a parrot perched on a ring.

MAKING YOUR OWN
BALANCING MAN.

In order to make your own Balancing Man, you will need: a large cork (33), three pieces of straight wire cut from a coat hanger—two measuring seven inches and one measuring 1½ inches (32), wire-cutting pliers (3), scissors (1), felt-tip pens (14), tape (8), a triangular file (5), lightweight cardboard (28), a ruler (4), and a spool of lightweight strong thread (35).

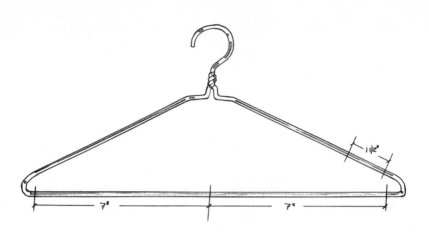

Cut two seven-inch and one 1½-inch pieces of wire from the coat hanger.

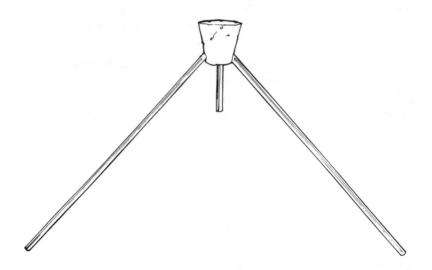

Insert the two seven-inch wires opposite each other in the cork as illustrated above. Then insert the 1½-inch wire in the center of the bottom of the cork.

If you wish, you can copy the pattern for the Balancing Man, which is provided below, onto the piece of cardboard.

Balancing-Man Pattern.

Cut out the acrobat and attach it to the top of the cork with either glue, tape, or a thumbtack.

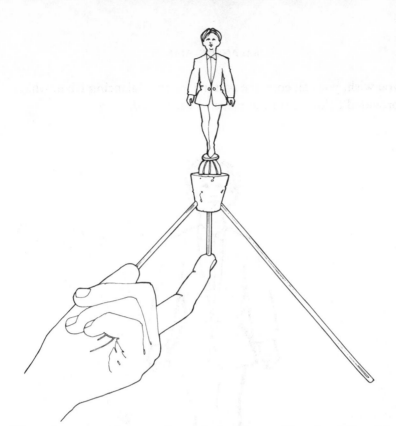

Place the toy on the top of your index finger. You should be able to balance it there without difficulty.

The Balancing Man can also be made to balance on a piece of strong thread. Using the small triangular file, make a small notch in the end of the 1½-inch piece of wire.

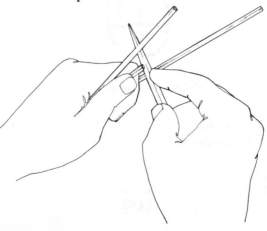

Now, string some thin but strong thread between two chairs.

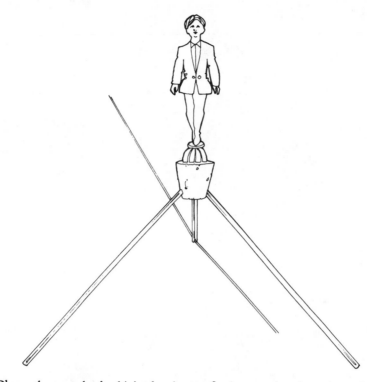

Place the notched 1½-inch piece of wire on the thread as shown above. The acrobat should keep his balance with ease. If you tilt the thread, the Balancing Man will also move down the thread just like an acrobat walking a tightrope.

SKYHOOK

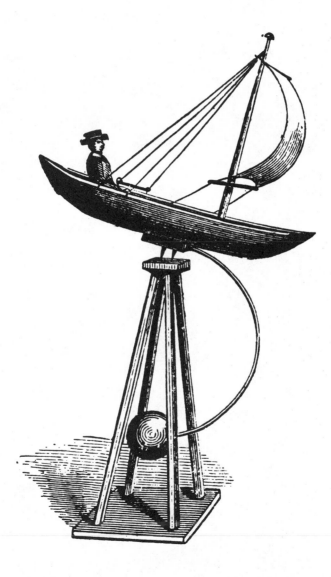

THE SKYHOOK is a traditional folk toy that has been in use for hundreds of years. During the nineteenth century the toy was commercially available in the forms of a man riding a horse and a sailor navigating a sailboat. They were essentially the same toy. Extending from both figures was a long, curved wire, at the end of which was set a counterweight. The center of gravity for the toy normally lay in the middle of the figure. A small balance point made of a piece of wire was then set in the figure. Set on the edge of a shelf or table with the wire and counterweight running underneath, the figure would precisely balance itself in what seemed to be an almost impossible manner.

HOW TO MAKE YOUR OWN SKYHOOK.

In order to make your Skyhook, you will need: a piece of lightweight cardboard 8½ by 11 inches (28), scissors (1), a pencil (13), pliers (3), tape (8), a wire coat hanger (32), and felt-tip pens (14).

Copy the pattern shown on the next page onto the piece of lightweight cardboard.

Once you have copied the pattern onto the cardboard, cut it out with the scissors. Now fold the pattern in half along the dotted line in the middle.

Skyhook Pattern.

If you wish, you may color in the pattern with the felt-tip pens.

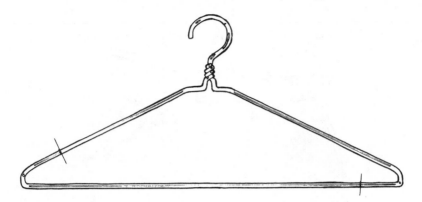

With the pliers, cut off a length of wire from the coat hanger as illustrated above. Throw away the section with the hook.

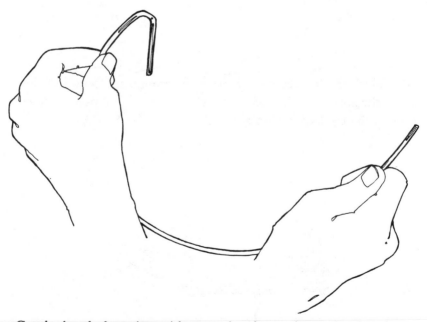

Gently bend the wire with your hands as shown in the above illustration.

Now punch the hooked end of the wire through the center of the fold at the bottom of the boat. It may be easier to first punch a hole through the cardboard with a pencil.

Tape the sails and the back of the boat together as shown above.

Set your Skyhook on the edge of a table or bookshelf. You can determine the way it balances by adjusting the angle of the boat by bending the piece of wire or by moving the cardboard. Once balanced, your Skyhook is complete!

ZOETROPE

THE ZOETROPE is an interesting variation and improvement on the Phantascope. Invented by W. G. Horner in 1834, the Zoetrope consists of a revolving drum with slits in its sides spaced at equal distances from one another. On the interior of the drum is a series of sequential pictures. These pictures appear to move when observed through the slits of the rotating drum. The device could be observed by many people at once, and it became an extremely popular parlor novelty and toy during the Victorian era. Variations on the Zoetrope included the Praxinoscope. Instead of using viewing slits, the Praxinoscope had a drum with a central hub to which mirrors were attached. These mirrors reflected each of the sequential pictures on the interior of the drum.

MAKING YOUR OWN
ZOETROPE.

In order to make your own Zoetrope, you will need: a piece of lightweight cardboard 8½ by 11 inches (28), felt-tip pens (14), tape (8), scissors (1), and an X-Acto knife (6).

Copy the patterns illustrated for this toy on the following pages onto the piece of cardboard.

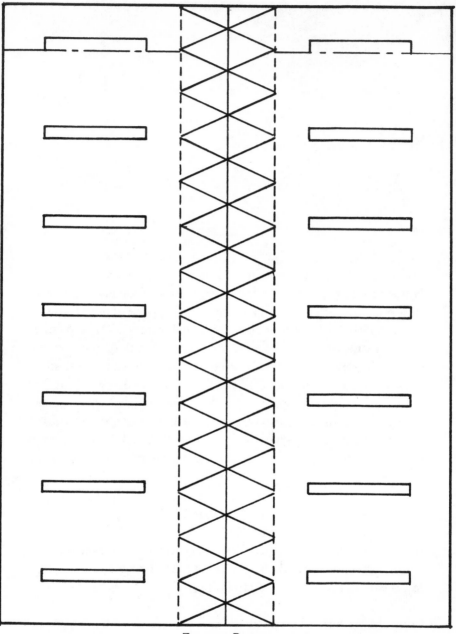

Zoetrope Pattern.

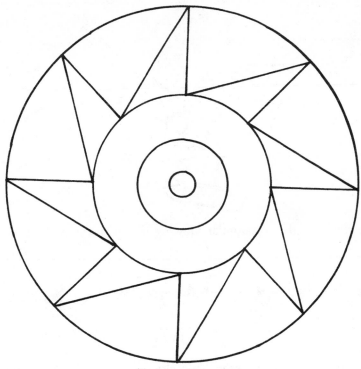

Zoetrope Pattern.

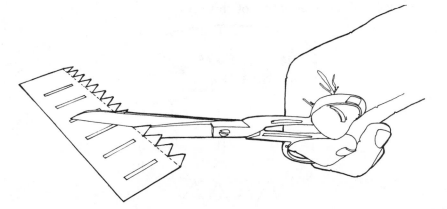

Cut the patterns out of the cardboard with the scissors.

Now cut out the rectangular viewing slits with the X-Acto knife.

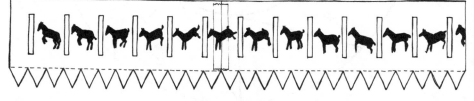

Tape the two strips together to make one long strip. Next draw a series of sequential pictures in the blank sections between each viewing slit. You can copy the sequential drawings of the donkey included with the description of this toy.

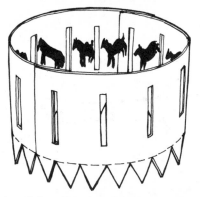

Now tape the ends of the strip together to make a circle.

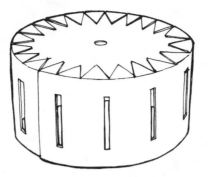

Fold over the jagged edge of the cardboard circle and tape it to the edge of the circular base as shown above. Punch a hole approximately one-eighth of an inch in diameter in the center of the base.

When your Zoetrope is finished, place it on a record turntable with the hole on the spindle. Turn on the turntable and view the pictures through the slits. If the turntable is set at 33⅓ rotations per minute, the pictures should appear to move. If you don't have a record player, you can put a pencil through the hole in the base of the Zoetrope and twirl it in order to see the moving pictures.

MAGIC LANTERN

THE MAGIC LANTERN'S princi-
ples were discovered, legend has it, by the thirteenth-century phi-
losopher and scientist Roger Bacon as part of his study of the
nature of shadows. Accused of being a product of witchcraft,
Bacon's lantern was eventually presented before Pope Innocent IV,
who declared it a harmless device that had nothing to do with the
devil.

Actual evidence for the existence of Magic Lanterns can be found
in engravings from the seventeenth century. These illustrations
show an oil lamp placed inside a box, a highly polished metal re-
flector that focuses the light, a painted slide through which the light
is shown, and a hole in the box through which the light is projected.

Throughout the seventeenth and eighteenth centuries, Magic Lantern showmen and wizards traveled all over Europe using the instrument to conjure up ghosts and frightful monsters. With the
invention of photography during the early nineteenth century, the
machine was greatly improved and its use widely expanded. Not
only did scientific lecturers use it to illustrate their presentations,
but it also became a popular parlor toy for exhibiting comic
pictures.

MAKING YOUR OWN
MAGIC LANTERN.

In order to make your own Magic Lantern, you will need: scissors (1), colored ball-point pens (15), a ruler (4), tape (8), a shoebox, a small piece of paper (24), a flashlight (17), and a magnifying glass.

For your Magic Lantern slides, you can use regular photographic slides or make your own with sheets of clear plastic (37) and colored ball-point pens.

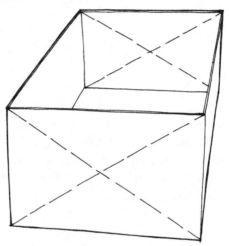

On each end of the bottom half of the shoebox, mark the center of the end, using the ruler and a pen.

Hold the circular end of the flashlight on each of these spots and draw around its edge to make a circle. Do this for both ends of the box. Now cut out both of these circles.

Next, trace the pattern illustrated on top of the next page (for the slide holder) onto the piece of paper.

Cut out the circle of the slide holder. Fold the paper along the dotted lines.

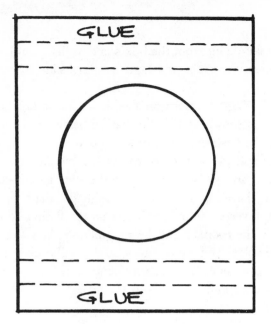

Slide-Holder Pattern.

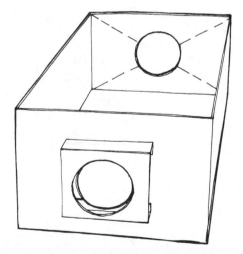

Put glue along the strips marked "glue" and glue the slide holder to one end of the shoebox so that the open circle is right in front of the circle already cut out of the box's end. The slide holder should sit out just a little bit from the box's end so that you have sufficient room to insert the slides or Magic Lantern slide strips.

Set up your Magic Lantern on a table or on the floor in front of a blank door as shown in the illustration below. Put the lid on the box. Place the flashlight on a book so that its beam is at the same level as the hole in the back of the box. Now put your slide in the slide holder. Always be sure to put the slide in upside down, because when the light is focused through the magnifying glass or lens, it will reverse the image. Turn on the flashlight and turn off the lights in the room. Hold the magnifying glass directly in front of the slide holder and move it toward the wall until the slide comes into focus. The slide will probably come into focus when the magnifying glass is about a foot from the slide.

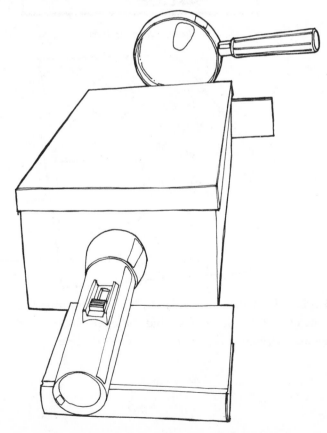

In order to make your own Magic Lantern slide strips, you will need to cut strips of clear plastic two inches wide and eight inches long.

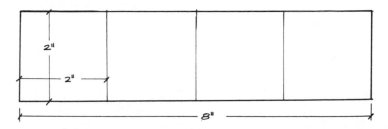

Divide each strip into two-inch squares. Each of these squares will be an individual slide frame. Draw a picture in the center of each frame. These may be different pictures or may tell a story like the ones illustrated in the pattern below.

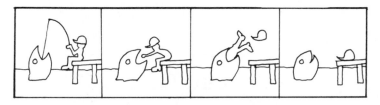

You can color the water blue with a colored ball-point pen, the pier brown, the fish black, the man's suit a dark blue, and his hat red.

As you slide the slide strip through the Magic Lantern slide holder be sure it is upside down. Pause at each frame and watch as you create a very simple moving picture!

MOVING SLIDES

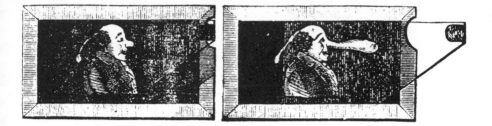

MOVING SLIDES were invented in the eighteenth century. In 1736, Pieter van Musschenbroek introduced a new version of the Magic Lantern. He was able to produce motion on a screen by using a painted glass slide as a background and moving another slide in front of it. When light was projected through the two slides, the image on the screen appeared to move.

Moving Slides became popular toys during the nineteenth century. Single Moving Slides were simply constructed and were very cheap. They could produce a great variety of amusing effects, such as elongation of noses, moving eyes, people dancing, and donkeys kicking. Sometimes light was provided by using a kerosene projector. You can make a Moving Slide show for yourself, using only clear plastic, paper, and a flashlight.

MAKING YOUR OWN
MOVING SLIDES.

To make your own Moving Slides, you will need: an envelope, scissors (1), tape (8), a sheet of white paper (24), a sheet of clear plastic (37), colored ball-point pens (15), and an X-Acto knife (6).

Along the bottom edge of the front of the envelope, measure a distance of four inches from the end. From that point, measure up two inches. Then mark a point on the outer edge of the envelope two inches up from the bottom.

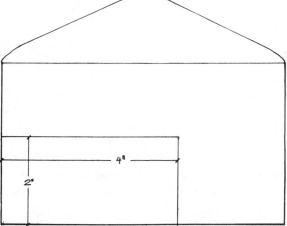

Draw a line connecting the points so that they form a rectangle measuring two by four inches.

Then cut along the line you have drawn so that you have a small envelope with the top and one side open.

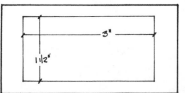

Draw a window three inches long and 1½ inches high in the middle of the new envelope.

With the X-Acto knife, cut the window out of both sides of the envelope.

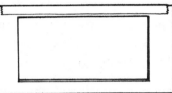

Next, tape the top of the envelope closed so that only one end is open.

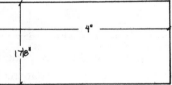

Cut a piece of white paper four inches long and 1⅞ inches high so that it will slip into the envelope.

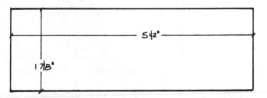

Now cut a piece of clear plastic 5½ inches long and 1⅞ inches high.

With the ball-point pens, draw on the piece of white paper a face without eyeballs to the left of the center.

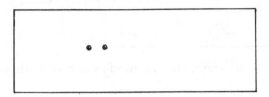

Next place the clear plastic over the drawing you have just made so that the left edges of the plastic and the paper are even. On the clear-plastic piece, draw two big eyeballs with the pen.

Now you are ready to put your Moving Slide together. Place the white piece of paper in the envelope so that the face shows through the window.

Then put the clear plastic strip in the envelope and over the picture.

As you pull the plastic in and out of the envelope, you will see a Motion Slide of the face's eyes moving from left to right.

If you wish to project your Moving Slide onto the wall, you will need to redraw the picture (the face without eyeballs) on a piece of plastic the same size as the piece of paper. Find a blank white wall or tape a piece of white paper to a wall of any color. Turn out the lights. Shine the light from a flashlight through the pieces of plastic in the envelope. If you adjust the light properly as you did for the Magic Lantern, an image will appear on the wall. Now ask a friend to move the longer piece of plastic back and forth while you hold the envelope and the flashlight. The image or picture projected on the wall will appear to move. You can also use the Magic Lantern itself to project the Moving Slides onto the wall.

REVOLVING
SERPENT

THE REVOLVING SERPENT is a simple toy that uses the same principle as that used for thermal devices, whose movement is based upon rising currents of hot air. Such devices have been in use since the time of the ancient Greeks. During the nineteenth century, a spinning metal disc with vanes was commonly placed on top of oil lamps to prevent the smoke of the lamp from rising in a direct column and blackening the ceiling.

Made from either paper or a thin sheet of copper, the Revolving Serpent was suspended by a string over the top of an oil lamp or hot stove. Hot air rising from either one of these sources would cause the toy to turn around and around.

MAKING YOUR OWN
REVOLVING SERPENT.

In order to make your own Revolving Serpent, you will need: a piece of paper (24), scissors (1), a pencil (13) or pen (14), a needle (9), and a ten-inch piece of lightweight thread (35).

Trace the pattern included for this toy on the opposite page onto the piece of paper.

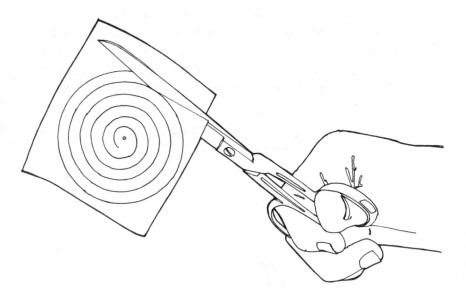

Cut the paper along the dotted line of the pattern. When you have finished cutting out the pattern, you will have a spiral.

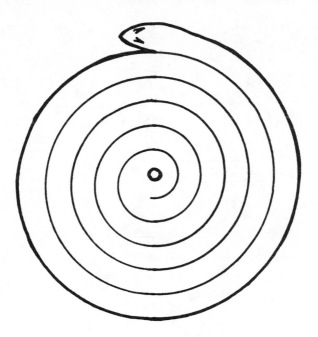

Revolving-Serpent Pattern.

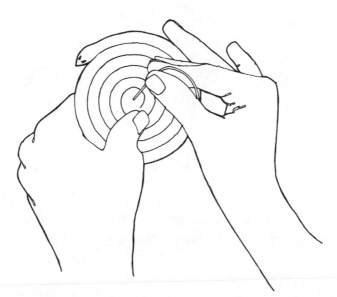

Make a knot in the end of the thread. Using the needle, poke the thread through the end of the serpent's tail.

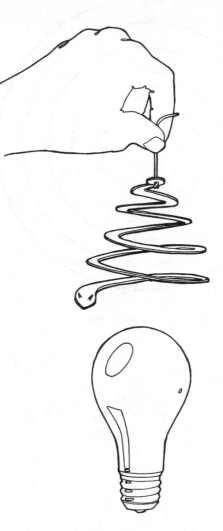

Now suspend the serpent by the thread a few inches above an electric light bulb. When you turn on the light, the serpent will slowly rotate as the heat from the bulb rises.

TUMBLER

THE TUMBLER was an extremely popular toy in England and America during the late nineteenth and early twentieth centuries. In Japan, a similar type of toy known as a Daruma has been played with by both children and adults for hundreds of years.

In most instances, Tumblers consist of a simple doll-figure with a rounded bottom that contains a counterweight. When the Tumbler is pushed over on its side, the weight in its bottom causes it to stand upright.

MAKING YOUR OWN
TUMBLER.

In order to make your own Tumbler, you will need: an uncooked egg, three to four tablespoons of salt or sand, a small bowl, a spoon, a pin (9), tape (8), glue (16), scissors (1), paper (24), and felt-tip pens (14).

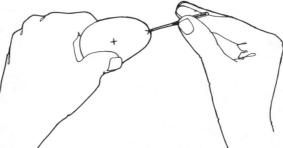

Take the pin and punch a hole about one-eighth of an inch wide at the small end of the egg. Then make a second hole about the same size in the middle of the egg (at the place so marked in the illustration). Be careful not to crack the egg by pushing too hard on its shell.

Place the egg over the bowl so that the hole in the middle is facing it. Now gently blow into the hole at the small end, forcing the contents inside the egg out the hole in the middle.

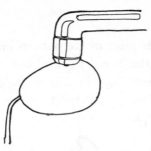

When you have blown everything out of the inside of the shell, gently run water from a faucet through the hole in the middle of the shell. Once the egg is full of water, blow it out the same way you blew out the contents of the egg. Repeat this process until the inside of the shell is clean.

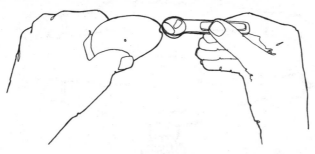

Once the shell has dried, spoon either some sand or salt into the top of the shell. Put in enough sand or salt so that the bottom of the shell is much heavier than the upper end.

Tape over the two holes in the egg. Then copy the pattern on the next page onto a piece of paper and cut it out. You can color the pattern with the felt-tip pens.

TUMBLER.

Fold the semi-circular piece of the pattern into a cone and glue it together. Next, fold the Tumber's head and arms along the dotted line and insert this piece into the slits in the cone. Glue these two pieces together and then tape the Tumbler onto the egg. Your Tumbler is now complete!

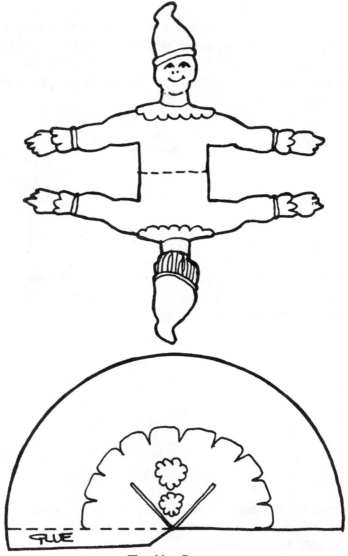

Tumbler Pattern.

MICROSCOPE

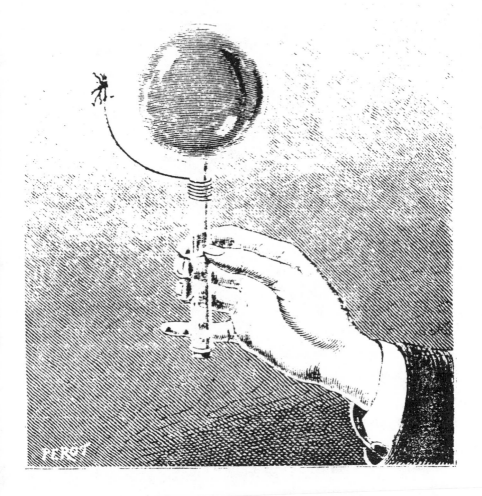

THE MICROSCOPE was invented about 1590 by a Dutch spectacle maker, Zacharias Janssen. One of his contemporaries, the Italian physicist Galileo, improved upon Janssen's design and was able to observe objects as complex and small as an insect's eye. Despite Galileo's success, it was the seventeenth-century Dutch scientist Anton van Leeuwenhoek who eventually developed the first practical modern Microscopes, which were capable of magnifying objects up to 300 times their original size.

During the eighteeenth and nineteenth centuries, various types of extremely simple Microscopes were used as toys. These Microscopes were most often simple pinhole constructions from cardboard or foil or were based upon the magnifying power of water, like the water-filled glass ball shown on page 157.

HOW TO MAKE TWO SIMPLE
MICROSCOPES.

In order to make your own Microscopes, you will need: a round plastic or cardboard pint- or quart-size ice-cream container, a clear plastic bag, some rubber bands, a piece of aluminum foil approximately three by three inches, a pin (9), scissors (1), and some water.

Cut out the bottom of the ice-cream container.

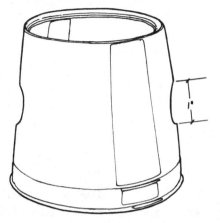

Then cut two holes, one inch in diameter, opposite each other on the sides of the container (in order to let in light). Cut the plastic along its seams so that you have a single thickness of plastic.

Now cover the top of the container loosely with the piece of plastic. Place the rubber bands around the plastic so that they hold it in place on the top of the container.

Slowly pour a small amount of water onto the plastic. The weight of the water will make the plastic sag, causing it to take the form of a lens.

Put various objects underneath the water lens. Experiment with different amounts of water, which will change the shape of the lens and will make it work more effectively.

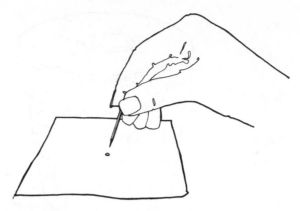

Another simple type of Microscope can be made by boring a small hole through a piece of aluminum foil with a pin.

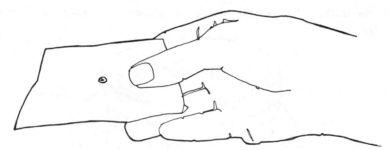

Drop a very small amount of water into the hole. Surface tension will keep the water from falling through the hole.

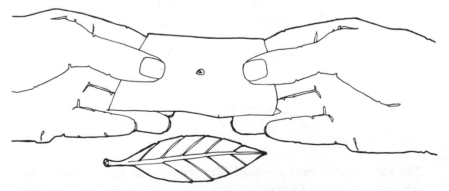

Place an object underneath the lens and examine it. If you use this type of Microscope, a magnification of 150 times the size of the object is possible!

HELICOPTER

No. 811,784.

PATENTED FEB. 6, 1906.

L. B. MATTESON.
FLYING TOY.
APPLICATION FILED FEB. 16, 1905.

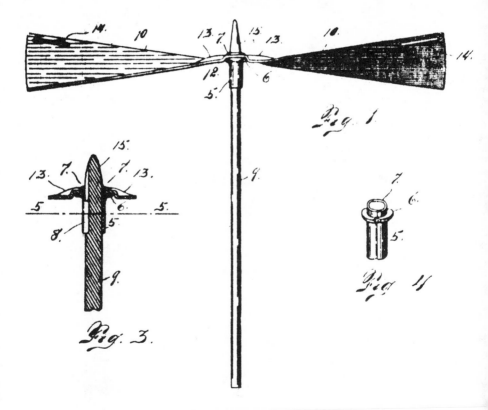

Helicopter toys have been made in many forms, but perhaps none is quite as simple or as effective as L. B. Matteson's "Flying Toy," illustrated on page 163. By placing your hands around the dowel and rubbing them together very hard in a counter-clockwise direction, it is possible to launch the Helicopter as high as thirty or forty feet into the air.

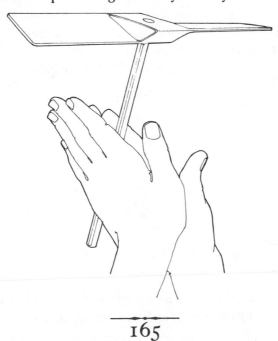

Boy with Helicopter Toy, c. 1584.

Matteson's "Flying Toy" is not a unique invention. Similar toys can be found in paintings and illustrations dating from the Renaissance.

MAKING YOUR OWN
HELICOPTER.

In order to make your own Helicopter, you will need: a piece of soft white pine eight inches by one inch by five-sixteenths of an inch (36), a dowel eight inches long and one-quarter of an inch in diameter (36), wood glue (16), a wood-carving knife (6), an electric or hand drill (7), and a medium grade of sandpaper (11).

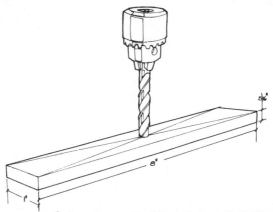

Mark the center of the piece of white pine and drill a hole one-quarter-inch in diameter perpendicular to the center mark.

Copy the above pattern onto a piece of paper and cut it out.

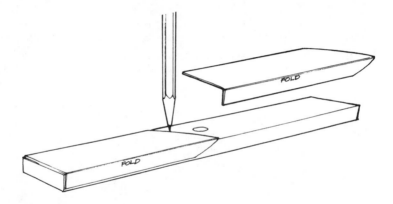

Place the pattern on the wood as shown above and trace around it. Repeat this process for all the corners.

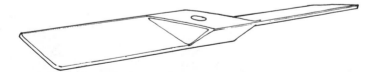

Carve a propeller out of the pine so that the plane of each side crosses as shown above.

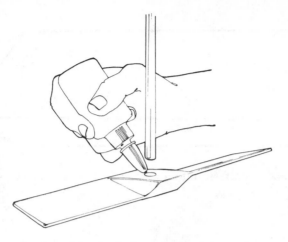

Now place the dowel in the hole and glue it into place, making sure that the propeller is exactly perpendicular to it.

Your Helicopter is now ready to fly!

HELICOPTER-PARACHUTE

THE HELICOPTER–PARACHUTE, a simple toy often made by nineteenth-century children, combined the principles of the parachute, outlined by Leonardo da Vinci, and those of the helicopter, of which Leonardo also made detailed designs. In nature, the same principle can be found at work with "Maple Spinners" and other types of airborne seed pods, and it may in fact have been the source of inspiration for this toy.

Leonardo da Vinci's Design for a Helix Vertical Take-off Device (Helicopter), 1490.

MAKING YOUR OWN HELICOPTER–PARACHUTE.

In order to make your own Helicopter–Parachute, you will need: a piece of paper 8½ by 11 inches (24) and scissors (1).

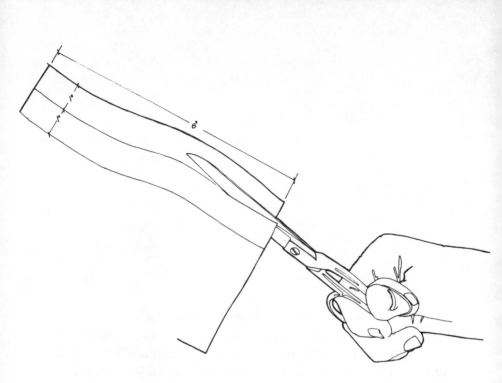

Using the scissors, cut out two strips of paper 8½ inches long and one inch wide.

Place the two strips of paper back to back and twist them together for approximately three or four inches.

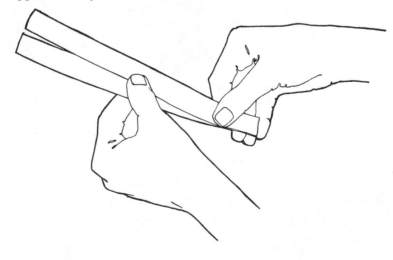

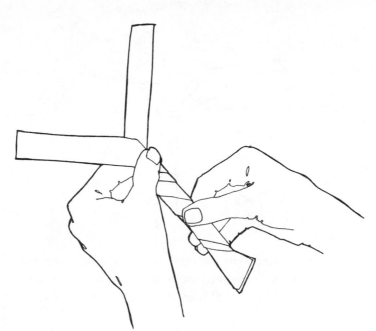

Now fold back the two unfolded ends of the paper strips so that they form the blades for the Helicopter–Parachute.

Bend each of the blades of the Helicopter–Parachute slightly in different directions. Test your Helicopter–Parachute by dropping it to the ground. Adjust the angle of the blades until they cause it to evenly spin or twirl to the ground.

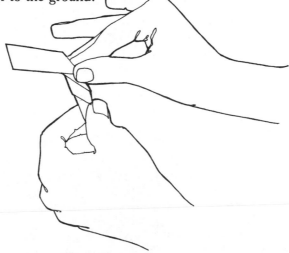

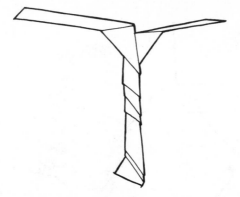

Your finished Helicopter–Parachute should look like this. If the Helicopter–Parachute drops too quickly, cut a small piece off of the bottom (twisted) part until it works exactly the way you want it to.

PAPER-WRESTLERS

THE PAPER-WRESTLERS are a
popular folk-toy that was also commercially manufactured and
sold during the second half of the nineteenth century. Their origins, however, are much older. In a manuscript from the twelfth
century, there is an illustration of two knights fighting each other
that are being manipulated by two men. It is clear that the Paper-
Wrestlers were a variation of these older Medieval knights. The
toy consists of two jointed figures, locked in combat with each
other, that are manipulated with strings held by the persons playing
with it. Despite its simplicity, the toy is exciting to play with.

HOW TO MAKE YOUR OWN
PAPER-WRESTLERS.

In order to make your own Paper-Wrestlers, you will need: a piece
of heavy thread (35) or lightweight string (34) approximately three
feet in length, five straight pins (9), a needle (9), scissors (1), a
piece of lightweight cardboard 8½ by 10 inches (28), and pliers (3).

Trace the pattern of the Paper-Wrestlers on the following page
onto the cardboard and cut them out.

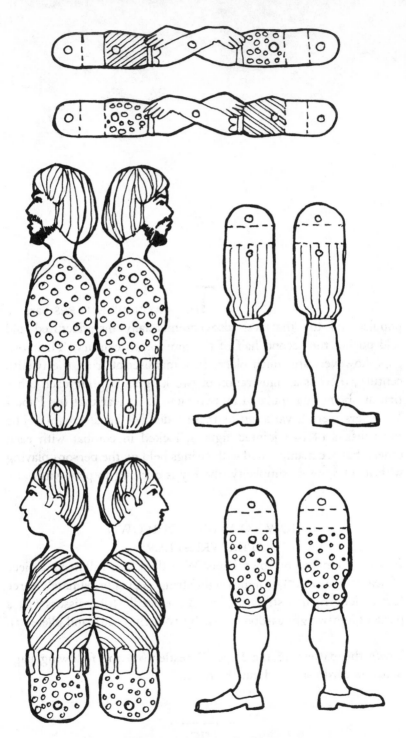

Paper-Wrestlers Pattern.

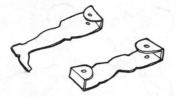

Bend the arms and legs along the dotted lines as illustrated above.

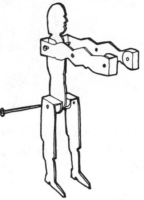

Attach the arms and legs to the bodies of the wrestlers by forcing a pin through the specially marked points.

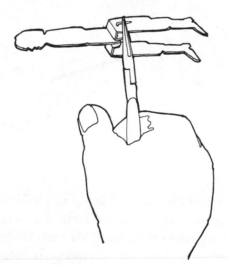

Bend the pointed tips of the pins down with the pliers.

Thread the piece of heavy thread or light string through a needle and use it to draw the thread through the points marked on the arms of the two figures.

Take the ends of each of the pieces of string and hold them in your hands. By moving your hands back and forth, you will be able to make the wrestlers appear to be fighting. By each holding a string, you and a friend can have a wrestling match with the Paper-Wrestlers!

PEEPSHOW

PEEPSHOWS have been popular toys for both children and adults since the Renaissance. The Italian artist Alberti supposedly made a Peepshow as early as 1437 to illustrate the principles of perspective. Peepshows can also be found dating from the seventeenth and eighteenth centuries. It was during the nineteenth century that they became most popular as a children's toy. The openings of the Thames Tunnel in 1828 and the Crystal Palace Exhibition in 1851 were popular subjects for Victorian Peepshows.

Peepshows, which were also called "Raree shows," consisted of a series of pictures and scenery arranged in a closed box that was viewed either through a large opening or a peep hole. Light entered the Peepshow through holes in the sides and top of the box. Colored-paper Peepshows that opened like an accordion were widely manufactured during the nineteenth century. Called "panoramas," these toys should not be confused with the moving panoramas described elsewhere in this book.

HOW TO MAKE YOUR OWN PEEPSHOW.

In order to make your own Peepshow, you will need: a shoebox or small cardboard box with its lid, lightweight cardboard (28) and paper (24), scissors (1), glue (16), and colored felt-tip pens (14).

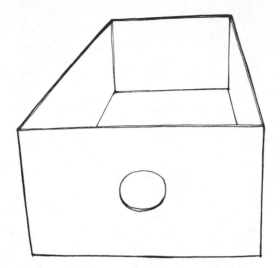

Remove the lid of the box. Cut a hole in the center of one of the ends of the box, approximately one inch in diameter.

Decide upon a subject for your Peepshow. One that emphasizes perspective or distance is best, such as a forest and distant mountains or a long and narrow room filled with furniture and people.

Cut pieces of scenery for the Peepshow out of the lightweight cardboard. Leave a narrow flap along the bottom of each piece of scenery in order to glue it to the floor of the Peepshow box. Draw individual sections of the scene on the different pieces of scenery. Color the scenery and the walls of the Peepshow box.

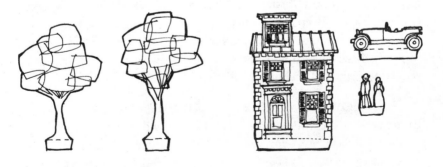

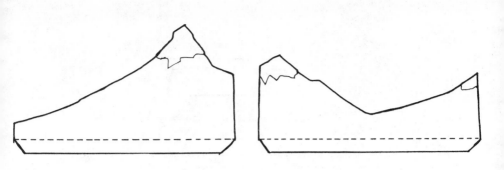

Glue the cut-out pieces of scenery into place.

Now cut holes in the lid of the box to let light in. You may also want to put holes in the sides of the box. A diffused or soft light works best for Peepshows. You can make this type of light by covering the holes with tracing paper. Colored lighting can be produced by covering the same holes with clear colored plastic or tissue paper.

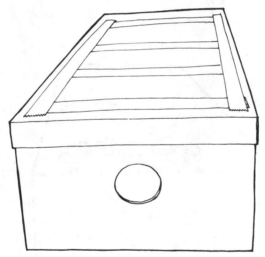

Put the lid back on top of the Peepshow box. Your Peepshow is now ready for viewing!

PARACHUTE

W. J. KUNTZSCH.

TOY PARACHUTE.

No. 384,533.   Patented June 12, 1888.

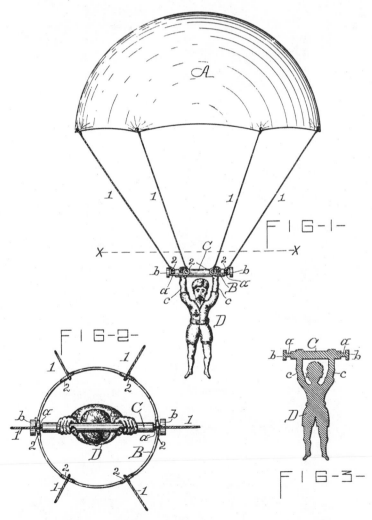

The PARACHUTE is said to have been invented by the Italian artist and inventor Leonardo da Vinci. How long children have played with parachutes as toys is not known, although we do have illustrations of their being played with by children as early as the middle of the eighteenth century.

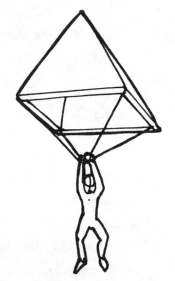

Leonardo da Vinci's Design for a Parachute, c. 1485.

MAKING YOUR OWN
PARACHUTE.

In order to make your own Parachute, you will need: a plastic bag (37), four pieces of lightweight string each 12 inches long (34), three or four heavy washers (18), and scissors (1).

Cut a square 12 by 12 inches out of the plastic bag.

Tie a piece of string to each corner of the plastic square.

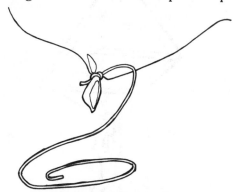

Now draw the end of all four strings together and tie them to the washers.

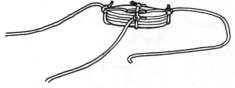

Your Parachute is ready to be launched. Fold the plastic square over on itself and place the washers on top. Make sure that the strings do not become tangled with one another.

Toss your folded Parachute into the air as high as you can and watch it float to the ground.

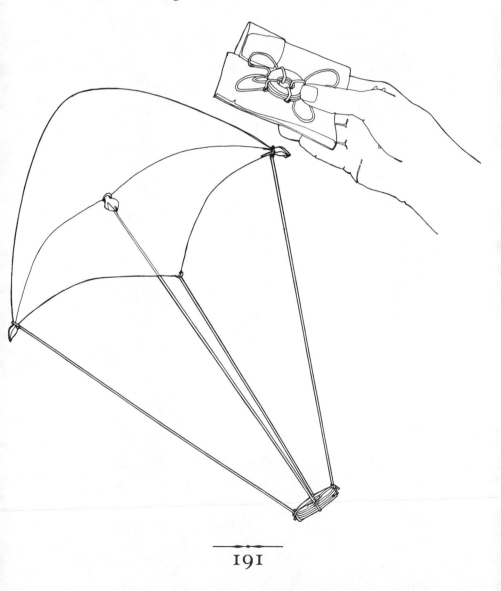

CUP AND BALL

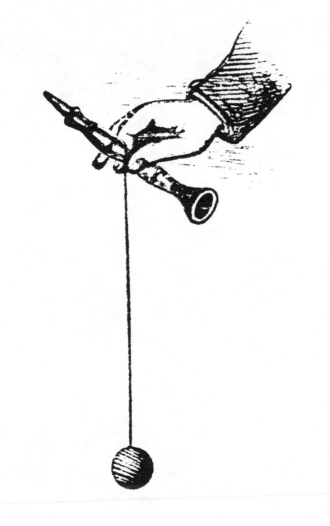

THE CUP AND BALL'S origin is unclear, but we know that the toy was well known in India and Greece very early and had become very fashionable as a toy among adults and children in Italy and France by the late sixteenth century. In France, the game was called *bilboquet*, a name derived from *bille,* meaning a wooden ball, and *bocquet*, the point of a spear. When Captain Cook visited the Sandwich Islands (Hawaii) in the eighteenth century, he found the natives playing simple versions of the game. By the early nineteenth century, the Cup and Ball could be found in the United States and Mexico and among the Canadian Eskimos.

Cup and Ball is a game that tests the hand-and-eye coordination of the player. Played indoors or out, the game usually consists of a cup made of wood or ivory. The shallower the cup, the more difficult the game. The solid ball was connected to the cup by a string. Sometimes the cup was attached to a handle. Another version of the game replaced the cup with a wooden spike, and the ball had a hole drilled through its center.

In order to play Cup and Ball, the players would hold the cup around its base and stretch their arms out so that the ball hung toward the ground. They would then swing their arms, causing the ball to fly out, and try to catch it in the cup as it fell back down. The version of the toy with a spike was much more difficult, since the ball had to be caught on the end of the spike.

MAKING YOUR OWN
CUP AND BALL.

In order to make your own Cup and Ball, you will need a styrofoam or small paper cup, a two-foot piece of string (34), a Ping-Pong ball, and a pencil (13).

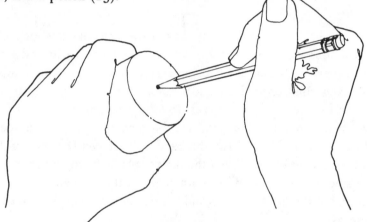

With the pencil, punch a hole in the center of the bottom of the cup.

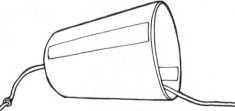

Thread the string through the hole from the inside of the cup and tie about three knots in the string on the bottom of the cup to hold the string in place.

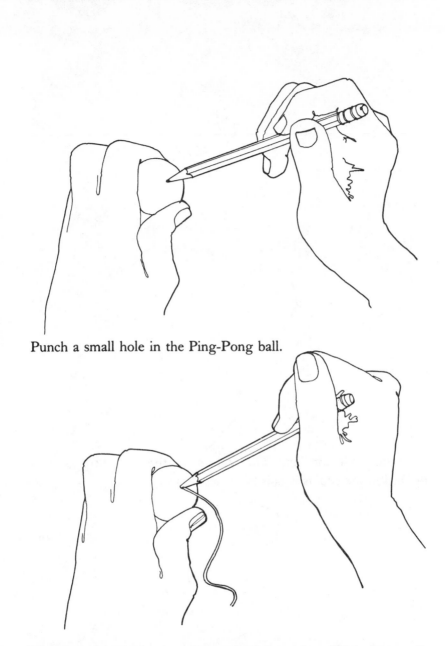

Punch a small hole in the Ping-Pong ball.

Tie several knots in the other end of the string. With the pencil, gently push the knotted end of the string through the hole in the Ping-Pong ball.

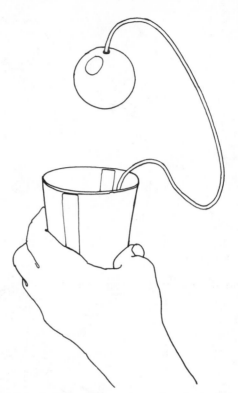

Hold the cup in one hand. Throw it up into the air and try to catch the ball in the cup as it falls back downward.

Once you have become good at playing the game with this-size cup, try cutting down its sides to make it more difficult to catch the ball.

BULLROARER

THE BULLROARER, or "Thunder-Spell," is among the most ancient and universal toys. In one form or another, Bullroarers have been found in cultures as diverse as those of the Eskimos, the Australian and New Zealand Aborigines, and the ancient Greeks and Britons. In its most common form, the Bullroarer consisted of a thin slat of wood tied to a long piece of string. When whirled rapidly around in the air, the device would make a loud noise—hence its name. Bullroarers would often be used as part of religious and magical ceremonies. The Bullroarer was a common nineteenth-century toy that was popular with children and often very unpopular with adults. An English author writing during the 1880s, for example, explained that he did not recommend it as a toy because:

> In the first place it makes a most horrible and unexampled din, which recommends it to the very young, but renders it detested by people of mature age. In the second place, the character of the toy is such that it will almost infallibly break all that is fragile in the house where it is used, and will probably put out the eyes of some of the inhabitants.

The Bullroarer is an excellent toy if used safely and away from grouchy adults!

MAKING YOUR OWN
BULLROARER.

In order to make your own Bullroarer, you will need: a piece of heavy string about 36 inches long (34), a piece of heavy cardboard measuring nine by two inches (28), and scissors (1).

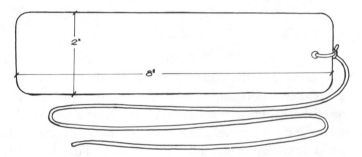

Cut out a piece of cardboard eight by two inches. Round off all four of the corners. Punch a hole one-half inch from one of the ends and thread the string through the hole. Knot the string tightly.

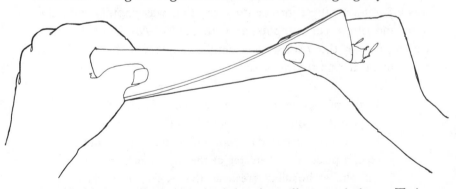

Next, hold the Bullroarer in both hands as illustrated above. Twist one end up and then down, just slightly, to give the surface a slight bend.

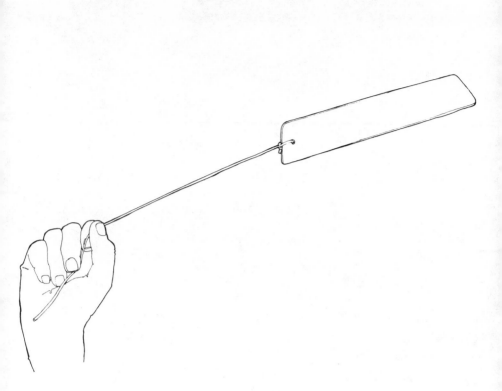

Your Bullroarer is now ready to use. Take it outside to a safe, open space and swing it in circles over your head. With a little experimenting, it will make a loud roaring noise.

AEOLIAN TOP

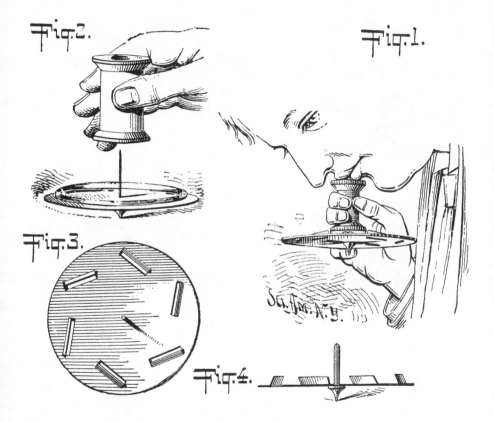

Fig.2.

Fig.1.

Fig.3.

Fig.4.

Sci. Am. N.Y.

THE AEOLIAN TOP is one of the most popular and simplest types of tops, which are among the oldest and most interesting of all toys. Heavily decorated tops made from wood and stone were popular in ancient Egypt; tops from Thebes made of fired clay have been found dating from 1200 B.C. Tops were also popular in both ancient Rome and China.

Technically, a top is defined as a revolving body that is held in equilibrium or balance on its vertical axis by its rotary motion. Historically, tops have taken many different forms. The whipping top, whose motion is maintained by its being lashed with a whip with knobs on its ends, was invented in ancient China and can be seen in European manuscripts dating from the fourteenth century. More-

The Whipping Top.

modern tops are driven by pull-strings, springs, wind power, and even electric motors.

Taking its name from the Greek god of the Wind, Aeolus, the Aeolian Top is propelled by the wind and was a popular toy during the late nineteenth century. It consists of a cardboard disc that has a series of oblique slots arranged symmetrically around its surface. These slots are cut out and turned up at right angles to the plane of the disc, forming wind vanes. A pin is set into the center of the disk and acts as a pivot for the top. Although not absolutely necessary, a thread spool was often used as a mouthpiece to set the top spinning. The spool was held to the mouth with the rounded end of the pin inserted in the hole at the base of the spool and held in place by the light pressure of a finger on the edge of the top disc. By blowing through the hole in the spool, a partial vacuum was created between the surface of the top and the spool. As soon as the blowing stopped, the top would drop and continue to revolve on its own momentum if on a flat surface.

MAKING YOUR OWN
AEOLIAN TOP.

In order to make your own Aeolian Top, you will need: a piece of lightweight cardboard (28), sealing wax or a candle, a straight pin (9), a small thread spool 1¼ inches tall (19), a pencil (13) and colored felt-tip pens (14), scissors (1), and an X-Acto knife (6).

Draw a circle approximately three inches across on the piece of cardboard. You can use the bottom of a glass or jar to make the circle, or you can copy the pattern on the opposite page. Be sure to draw the six diagonal flaps as shown in the pattern.

Cut out the circle with the scissors.

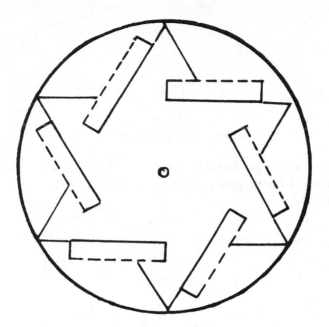

Aeolian-Top Pattern.

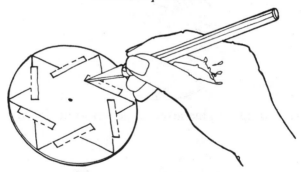

Now, cut along the three sides of the flaps with the X-Acto knife as shown above.

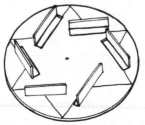

Bend up the flaps as shown above. Color the designs with the felt-tip pens.

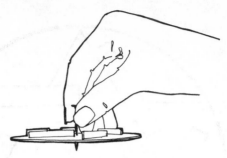

Stick the straight pin through the center of the disc, leaving about one-quarter-inch projecting below. This will serve as the pivot point for the top.

Apply several drops of glue around the pin to hold it in place.

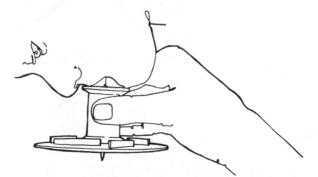

Now you are ready to play with your Aeolian Top. Hold the disc lightly against one end of the spool with your finger, letting the long end of the pin stick up through the hole in the spool. Blow through the other end of the spool. The stream of air you are making will spin the top rapidly and create a vacuum that will hold it against the spool.

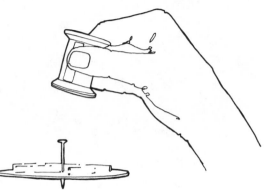

If you hold the whirling top over a table or any flat surface and stop blowing, it will drop from the spool and continue spinning!

JACOB'S LADDER

The Jacob's Ladder was an extremely popular folk-toy during the late nineteenth century, and it is still played with by children today. The toy takes its name from the *Bible*, the Book of Genesis, 28:12, in which there is a description of a dream of the prophet Jacob, who saw a ladder extending from earth to heaven on which angels could be seen coming and going.

The design of the Jacob's Ladder is extremely simple. Basically, a chain of thin wooden blocks are connected to one another by means of cloth tape. The tape is attached to the pieces of wood in such a way that an illusion is created of the wooden blocks' tumbling or falling over one another when the toy is used.

HOW TO MAKE YOUR OWN
JACOB'S LADDER.

In order to make your Jacob's Ladder, you will need: ten pieces of plywood or masonite, each piece two by two inches square and one-quarter-inch thick (36), sandpaper (11), approximately 15 feet of flat cloth tape one-half-inch wide (31), scissors (1), glue (16), and a hammer (2).

Sand all of the edges of the blocks of wood so that they are smooth.

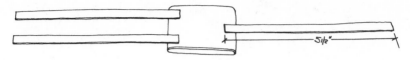

Cut the tape into 5½-inch lengths and glue the pieces of tape to the blocks as shown above. Leave one block without any tape.

Once the glue has dried, wrap the tapes around the blocks and line them up as shown below.

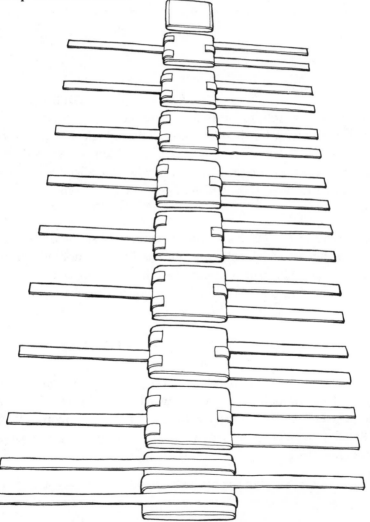

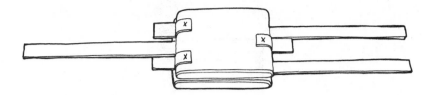

Stack block number 2 (cloth tape down) on top of block number 1 (cloth tape up). Trim and glue the pieces of tape from number 1 so that they can be attached at the points marked with *x*s on block 2 as illustrated above.

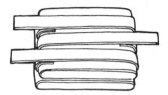

When the glue is dry, wrap the pieces of cloth tape over block number 2 as shown above.

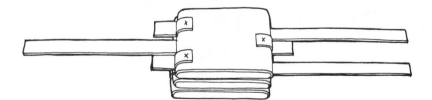

Stack block number 3 (cloth tape down) on top of block number 2 (cloth tape up) and glue the tape from block number 2 as indicated by the *x*s on block 3 in the illustration above. Repeat this process for all of the blocks that you have gotten together for your Jacob's Ladder.

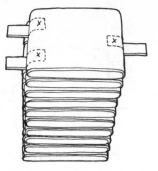

Wrap the cloth tapes on block number 9 and add the final blank block. Then glue the tapes as shown above.

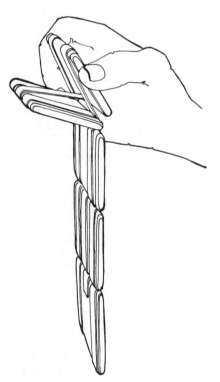

In order to work your Jacob's Ladder, hold the top block by its edge and tip it to touch the second block. This will trigger the tumbling action of the other blocks as you tip the top block back and forth.

CHANGEABLE
PORTRAITS

CHANGEABLE PORTRAITS were a popular toy for both children and adults during the Victorian era. The portraits were extremely simple in principle but could be constructed in many different ways by the person playing with them.

In most instances, Changeable Portraits consisted of a series of pictures divided into three separate parts. A collection of different portraits would be packed together in a boxed set. By removing any of the three parts of the picture and exchanging it for another card, a new portrait could be made. The addition of new cards gradually expanded the possible number of combinations that could be put together. An interesting variation on Changeable Portraits in the nineteenth century was a type of spelling puzzle in which the correct spelling and putting together of a word would provide the viewer with an assembled picture of the object spelled!

MAKING YOUR OWN
CHANGEABLE PORTRAITS.

To make your own Changeable Portraits, you will need: three or more three- by five-inch white cards (25), scissors (1), a ruler (4), and a pencil (13) or a felt-tip pen (14).

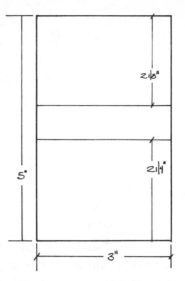

On each three- by five-inch card, draw a line 2⅛ inches from one end and another 2¼ inches from the other end so that each card is divided into three parts.

The top part of the card will be the forehead, the middle part the nose, and the lower part the mouth and chin of your faces.

It is very important to try to draw the eye, nose, mouth, and chin of each of the faces on the same place on each card so that they will match up with one another as you change the faces.

On the next page there are three patterns of faces that you may copy, or you may draw your own faces.

After you have drawn all the faces on your cards, cut along the lines that divide each card into three parts. Now you have all the parts of your Changeable Portraits. You can start mixing them up to make many, many different faces.

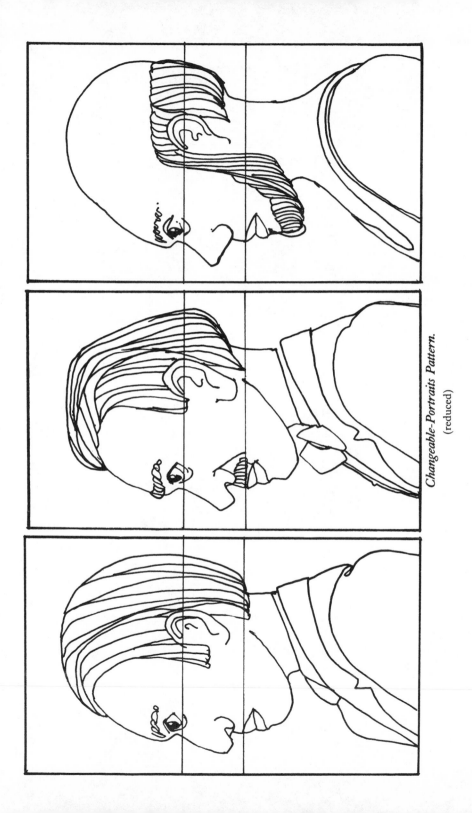

Changeable-Portraits Pattern.

(reduced)

PANORAMA

A PANORAMA is a picture or series of pictures that creates a continuous story that is unrolled before the spectator, one scene at a time. Invented in 1785 by Robert Barker, a Scottish artist, the Panorama was first presented before public audiences in 1788.

By the nineteenth century, small toy Panoramas had become popular as a means of telling the stories of famous European and American military battles and historical events. These toy Panoramas usually consisted of a strip of pictures that was gradually unrolled within a box. A large hole was cut in the front of the box for viewing and the scenes were often lighted from behind or above by candles. Toy Panoramas were often made by children.

MAKING YOUR OWN
PANORAMA.

In order to make your own Panorama, you will need: a shoebox, two cardboard tubes from foil, wrapping-paper, or waxed-paper rolls (30), a piece of lightweight cardboard (28), scissors (1), tape (8), plain white paper (24), and colored felt-tip pens (14) or crayons

(20). You may also use pictures from old magazines, if you wish, to make your Panorama story.

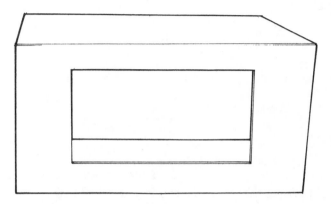

Remove the lid of the shoebox and cut a viewing window in the bottom.

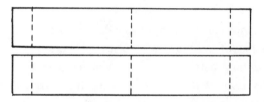

Cut two strips of lightweight cardboard at least six inches long and one-quarter-inch narrower than the width (diameter) of the cardboard tubes.

Bend each strip in the middle to form axles for the cardboard tubes. Next, bend up one-half-inch on each end of the axles to form flaps that will be taped to the floor of the Panorama box.

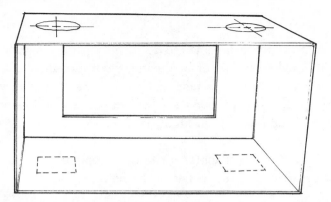

Mark two points on the floor of the Panorama box to indicate the position of the cardboard axles and tubes.

Cut out two holes, at least one-quarter-inch wider in diameter than the cardboard tubes, directly above these marks.

Spread the cardboard axles apart as shown above. Be sure that at their bottoms they are slightly narrower than the diameter of the cardboard tubes.

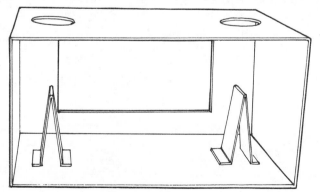

Tape the cardboard axles in place at the points marked on the floor of the Panorama box.

You can make the Panorama movie strip by pasting together pictures from old magazines or by creating your own story on a strip of white paper. It is important that each scene of the story is as wide as the Panorama window so that one scene at a time will appear as you roll the strip through the box.

The story roll for the Panorama can be as long as you like, but it cannot be wider than the height of the box.

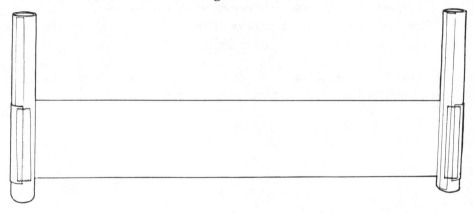

Tape one end of the story roll to one cardboard tube and the other end to the other tube. The pictures that make up the roll should be on the outside of the tubes.

Roll up the story roll so that the first scene is the only one showing.

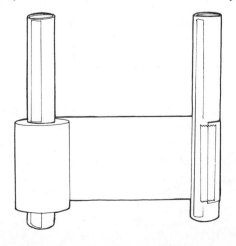

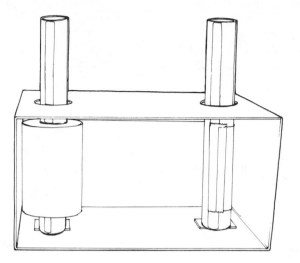

Slip the story roll and tubes in through the open back of the Panorama box. Stick the top ends of the tubes up through the holes. Now fit the lower ends down over the axles. You are ready to exhibit your Panorama!

Place the Panorama box on a table with its front well lighted, facing the audience. Turn the tubes evenly, pausing at each scene. You may also want to give a brief description of each scene to complete the story.

PINWHEEL

(No Model.)

C. A. MONTGOMERY.
PIN WHEEL BLANK.

No. 546,456.   Patented Sept. 17, 1895.

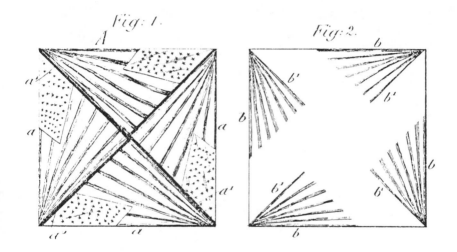

Fig. 1.   Fig. 2.

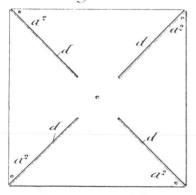

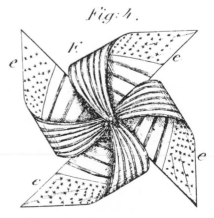

Fig. 3.   Fig. 4.

THE PINWHEEL'S principle is the same as that of the vertical windmill, which has been used for centuries in Europe to drive watermills and grind grain. Much smaller windmills became popular in the United States during the nineteenth century to pump water for livestock and homes and for irrigation purposes.

The windmill works by converting the linear motion of the wind into rotary motion, which turns its shaft. The turning force is transmitted by gears from the shaft to the parts of the machine that perform the work. Although the windmill itself faces the wind, its sails do not stand flat toward the wind, but at a slant, so that when the wind touches them they spin around.

The principle of the action of a windmill can be illustrated by the very simplest type of windmill, the Pinwheel, which is actually a windmill toy. Windmill toys were not models of windmills but usually consisted of the sails of a windmill fastened to a long stick. Woodcuts dating from the Middle Ages show boys and girls playing with these toys, usually made of wood or iron. Using paper, you can make a Pinwheel toy at home that is just like those sold at the fairs and circuses in England and America.

A Windmill Seller.

MAKING YOUR OWN
PINWHEEL.

In order to make a Pinwheel, you will need: a ten-inch-square piece of white paper (24), scissors (1), a thumbtack (21), a pencil (13), and a ruler (4). You may use crayons (20) or felt-tip pens (14) to decorate your Pinwheel.

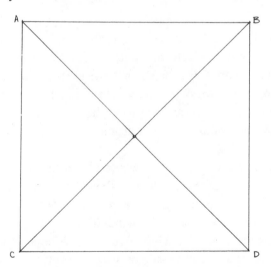

Using the ruler and pencil, draw two straight lines connecting the four corners of the square of paper as shown above. Label the four corners A, B, C, and D with your pencil. These two lines will cross at the center point of the square.

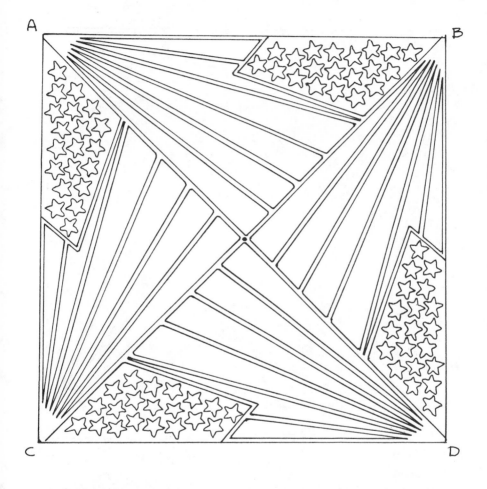

Copy the design shown above onto the square of paper. You can make the stars red and the strips blue or make up your own design.

The square of paper is larger than the pattern, so enlarge the designs as necessary.

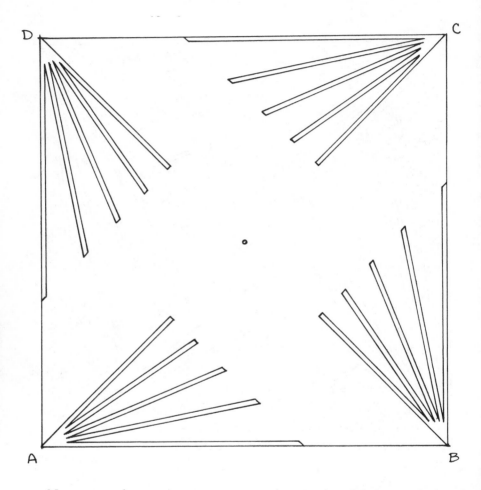

Now, turn the paper square over and copy the above pattern in blue. Place the square so that the A corner on the underside of the square is in the lower left corner and B is in the lower right corner.

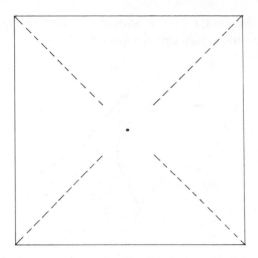

With the scissors, cut along the diagonal creases of the square from the corners to within one inch of the center.

Fold the corner pieces that are marked with the blue lines over to the center as shown above so that all four folded-over pieces are also marked with blue lines. Push a thumbtack through the corners and through the center of the square of paper. Next, push the thumbtack into the eraser tip of a pencil.

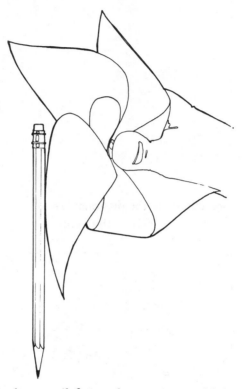

When you push the pencil forward as you run with it extended in front of you, the Pinwheel will whirl just as a real windmill turns. The faster you run, the faster the windmill Pinwheel will turn!

PERISCOPE

A PERISCOPE is an optical device that enables observers to view objects not directly in their line of vision. A simple Periscope consists of two parallel mirrors attached at 45° angles to the opposite ends of a tube.

It is not known who actually invented the Periscope. One of the first times it was used was during the Civil War. By the first World War, Periscopes were being used in submarines. Today they are used in industry and medicine in order to inspect hard-to-get-at surfaces. Periscopes have also been popular toys used to peer over walls and around corners and even to enable people to see over a crowd when watching a parade.

MAKING YOUR OWN
PERISCOPE.

In order to make your own Periscope, you will need: two quart-size milk cartons, two strips of lightweight cardboard 2¾ inches wide and 9¼ inches long (28), two small mirrors two to three inches long and two inches wide (29), a ruler (4), tape (8), scissors (1), and a pencil (13).

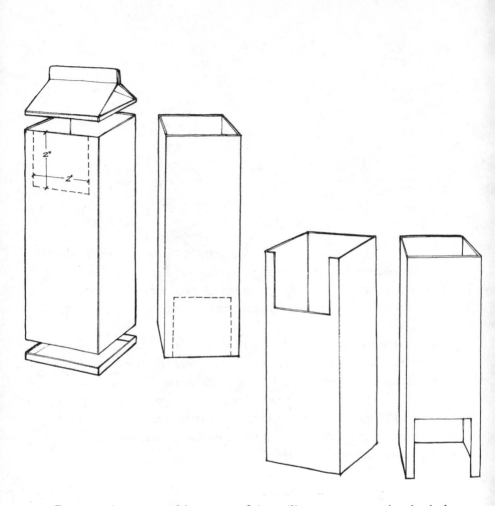

Remove the tops and bottoms of the milk cartons to make the hollow casing for the Periscope. Wash out the cartons and carefully dry them.

Measure a square two by two inches at the top of one of the sides of the cartons. Measure another square the same size on the second carton. Cut out these squares.

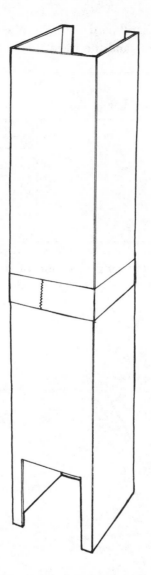

Tape the two milk cartons together so that one window is at the top and the other window is on the opposite side at the bottom of the casing.

Divide the strips of cardboard into three sections: Two should measure 2¾ inches long and the third should be 3¾ inches long.

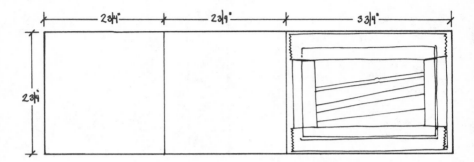

Tape each mirror to the longer section of these strips. Carefully crease each section of the cardboard in order to make it easier to fold.

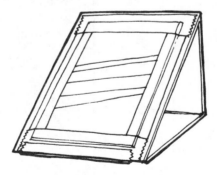

Fold the two strips of cardboard into triangles as illustrated above. Tape the open ends of the triangles together.

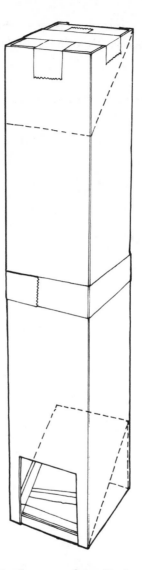

Slip one triangle into the bottom of the Periscope casing so that the mirror is opposite the window. Secure it in place by taping it across the bottom.

Slip the second triangle into the casing so that you see the mirror through the other window. Tape the triangle across the bottom to secure it in place.

Your Periscope is now ready to use to spy over walls and around corners!

BUBBLE
BLOWERS

BUBBLE BLOWERS have proba-
bly been used by children and adults since soap was invented by the
Sumerians in approximately 3000 B.C. Like many simple things,
they have a uniqueness and beauty that have often been taken too
much for granted. During the nineteenth century, numerous different types of pipes and frames for blowing bubbles were sold as toys.

In blowing bubbles, whether one uses a pipe or a wire frame the
same remarkable phenomenon occurs. Although the bubble can be
an elongated elliptical shape while it is being blown, it will not re-
tain this form. Because of surface tension, which makes the surface
of the bubble contract as much as possible, the soap bubble will
form the shape that encloses a given volume with a minimum
amount of surface area—the shape of a sphere.

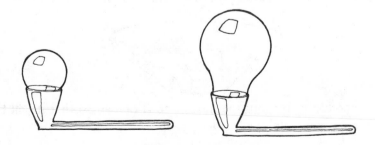

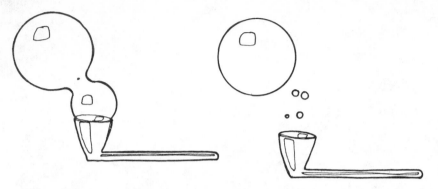

This simple but remarkable principle accounts for why the Earth and all of the other planets are globes or spheres.

Soap bubbles are unusual for a number of reasons that should be carefully noted. They can act as prisms for light and can reflect almost any color in the spectrum. They are also among the thinnest objects to be found in nature. According to the seventeenth-century English physicist Sir Issac Newton, at its thinnest point a soap bubble's membrane measures no more than 1/2,500,000 of an inch thick!

MAKING YOUR OWN
BUBBLE BLOWER
AND BLOWING BUBBLES.

In order to make and blow your own bubbles, you will need: a small mixing bowl or shallow pan, liquid detergent, a plastic funnel, a soda straw (12) or an old pipe, and scissors (1).

Pour enough water into the mixing bowl or pan so that it will be filled approximately one-half-inch deep.

Add a couple of strong squirts of liquid detergent.

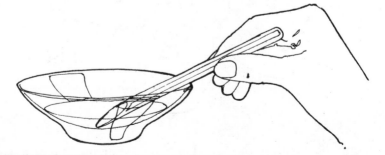

Cut the end of a soda straw at an angle as illustrated above.

Now gently dip the cut end of the straw into the soapy solution.

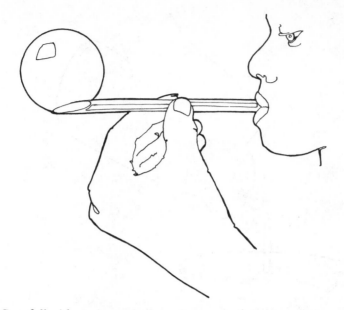

Carefully blow through the other end of the straw. A soap bubble should slowly appear!

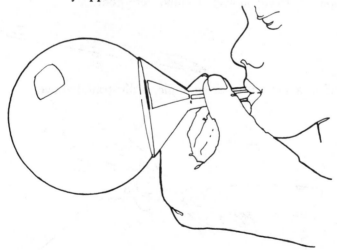

Using the mouth of the funnel or the bowl of an old pipe to collect the soap, you should be able to blow bubbles the same way.

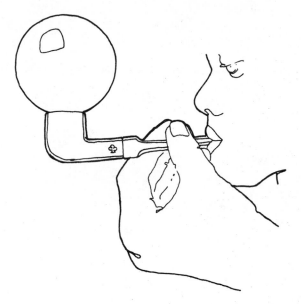

If you want your soap bubbles to last longer, you can buy some glycerine at the drugstore and mix it in with the soap solution. Add just enough glycerine to make the solution feel sticky.

HISTORICAL ILLUSTRATIONS (SOURCES)

The historical illustrations used in *The Historian's Toybox* are drawn primarily from works published during the nineteenth century. In addition to children's magazines and books, sources for the illustrations include patents and scientific journals, as well as specialized scientific monographs. The following references will, we hope, be of use to those interested in doing further research on the history of childhood and the history of toys.

ii ★ Early Victorian Toys Illustrating the Principles of Movement. From Twynihoe William Erle, *Science in the Nursery* (London, 1884) in Leslie Daiken, *Children's Toys Throughout the Ages* (New York: Frederick A. Praeger, 1953), p. 32, fig. 12.

11 ★ Thaumatrope. Gaston Tissandier, *Les Récréations Scientifiques* (Paris: G. Masson, Editeur, 1881), p. 111.

19 ★ Kite-Ferry. *St. Nicholas Magazine*, Vol. XXVII: No. 12 (October, 1900), p. 1074.

21 ★ Drawing based upon "The flyaway under full sail, moving upward on the kite-string," *St. Nicholas Magazine*, Vol. XXVII: No. 12 (October, 1900), p. 1073.

27 ★ Phantascope. *Scientific American*, November 26, 1881, p. 338.

33 ★ Tumbling Acrobat. *Scientific American,* April 30, 1892, p. 281.

39 ★ Marble Maze or Nerve Tester. *Scientific American,* April 16, 1887, p. 245.

41 ★ Drawings of labyrinth puzzles from Greek coins based upon illustrations in Mrs. F. Nevill Jackson, *Toys of Other Days* (New York: Scribner's Sons, 1908), p. 224.

45 ★ Kaleidoscope. Henry René D'Allemagne, *Histoire des Jouets* (Paris: Librairie Hachette & Co., 1902), p. 37.

53 ★ Boomerang. *Scientific American,* January 29, 1887, p. 72.

55 ★ Drawing based upon an Australian's throwing a boomerang in John D. Champlin and Arthur E. Bostwick, *The Young Folks Cyclopedia,* 2nd. Rev. ed. (New York: Henry Holt & Co., 1899), p. 103.

59 ★ Pneumatic Pea-Shooter. *St. Nicholas Magazine,* Vol. X: No. 12 (October 1883), p. 948.

63 ★ Three-Way Picture. Gaston Tissandier, *Popular Scientific Recreations,* trans. Henry Frith (New York: Ward, Lock and Co., 1890[?]), Chapter 1, Supplement, p. 11.

69 ★ Chromatrope Toys. T. J. W. Robertson, "Toy-Chromatropes," U.S. Patent No. 165,123. Patented June 29, 1875.

77 ★ Jumping Jack. *St. Nicholas Magazine,* Vol. VI: No. 4 (February 1879), p. 268.

85 ★ Floating Ball. Arthur Good, *La Science Amusante,* Troisième Série; 100 Nouvelle Expériences. Tom Tit (pseud.) (Paris: Librairie Larousse, 1906), p. 51.

89 ★ Sequential Pictures. *Scientific American,* October 16, 1878, p. 239.

93 ★ The Buzz. *Scientific American,* February 19, 1887, p. 120.

99 ★ Pandean Pipes. *Scientific American,* February 19, 1887, p. 120.

105 ★ Balancing Man. Twynihoe William Erle, *Science in the Nursery; or Children's Toys, and What They Teach* (New York: E. P. Dutton, 1884), p. 78.

113 ★ Skyhook. Twynihoe William Erle, *Science in the Nursery; or Children's Toys, and What They Teach* (New York: E. P. Dutton, 1884), p. 88.

121 ★ The Zoetrope, or Wheel of Life. *Milton Bradley Co.'s Catalogue* (Springfield, Massachusetts, 1884–85), p. 34.

129 ★ Magic Lantern. Gaston Tissandier, *Les Récréations Scientifiques* (Paris: G. Masson, Editeur, 1881), p. 351.

137 ★ Moving Slides. Samuel Highley, *The Popular Recreator,* Vol. II, p. 48, figs. 4 and 5.

145 ★ Revolving Serpent. *The American Boy's Book of Sports and Games* (New York: Dick & Fitzgerald, 1864), p. 525.

151 ★ Tumbler. Twynihoe William Erle, *Science in the Nursery; or Children's Toys and What They Teach* (New York: E. P. Dutton, 1884), p. 53.

157 ★ Microscope. Gaston Tissandier, *Les Récréations Scientifiques* (Paris: G. Masson, Editeur, 1881), p. 72.

163 ★ Helicopter. L. B. Matteson, "Flying Toy," U.S. Patent No. 811,784. Patented February 6, 1906.

166 ★ Drawing based upon an English print of children at play, c. 1584.

169 ★ Helicopter–Parachute. Arthur Good, *La Science Amusante,* Deuxième série; 100 Nouvelles Expériences. Tom Tit (pseud.) (Paris: Librairie Larousse, 188?), p. 189.

171 ★ Drawing based upon Helix vertical take-off device designed by Leonardo da Vinci, c. 1490.

175 ★ Paper-Wrestlers. "Hortus Deliciarum" by Herrade de Landsperg. Detail. *Scientific American Supplement,* #461 (November 1, 1884), p. 7362.

181 ★ Peepshow. *St. Nicholas Magazine,* Vol. X: No. 11 (September, 1883), p. 871.

187 ★ Toy Parachute. W. J. Kuntzsch, "Toy Parachute," U.S. Patent No. 384,533. Patented June 12, 1888.

189 ★ Drawing of parachute based upon Leonardo da Vinci's design for a parachute, c. 1485.

193 ★ Cup and Ball. *The American Boy's Book of Sports and Games* (New York: Dick & Fitzgerald, 1864), p. 464.

199 ★ Bullroarer. Arthur Good, *La Science Amusante,* Troisième Série; 100 Nouvelle Expériences. Tom Tit (pseud.) (Paris: Librairie Larousse, 1906), p. 93.

205 ★ An Air-Propelled Top. *Scientific American,* July 2, 1892, p. 4.

207 ★ Drawing based upon "Whipping the Town Top," in Mrs. F. Nevill Jackson, *Toys of Other Days* (New York: Scribner's Sons, 1908), p. 240.

213 ★ Jacob's Ladder. *Scientific American,* October 12, 1889, p. 227.

219 ★ Changeable Portraits of Ladies, 1819. Leslie Daiken, *Children's Toys Throughout the Ages* (New York: Frederick A. Praeger, 1953), p. 29, fig. 9.

225 ★ Panorama. *St. Nicholas Magazine.* Vol. X: No. 12 (October 1883), p. 945.

233 ★ Pinwheel. C. A. Montgomery, "Pinwheel Blank," U.S Patent No. 546,456. Patented September 17, 1895.

236 ★ Drawing based upon an engraving of the Windmill Seller by Poisson, 1774.

241 ★ The Zeiss Stereoscopic Field Glass. *Scientific American,* March 6, 1897, p. 148.

249 ★ Bubble Blowing. *Scientific American Supplement,* #495 (June 27, 1885), p. 7902.

INDEX

EUGENE F. PROVENZO, JR., a professor in the School of Education, University of Miami, is a specialist in the history of childhood and education. Not only is he interested in nineteenth- and early twentieth-century science, toys, and boardgames as a historian, but he has also designed award-winning toys.

ASTERIE BAKER PROVENZO is currently working on a history of the Dade County public schools. Her interest in toys is an outgrowth of research she has conducted on the history of childhood and education. She has co-authored books with her husband, Eugene, on family and community history, board games, and nineteenth-century science.

PETER A. ZORN, JR., is an associate professor teaching graphic design and illustration at the University of Miami. He has wide-ranging experience in production, design, development, and screenwriting. He has collaborated with the Provenzos on many books, including a series of paper models.

A CATALOG OF SELECTED
DOVER BOOKS
IN ALL FIELDS OF INTEREST

A CATALOG OF SELECTED DOVER
BOOKS IN ALL FIELDS OF INTEREST

CONCERNING THE SPIRITUAL IN ART, Wassily Kandinsky. Pioneering work by father of abstract art. Thoughts on color theory, nature of art. Analysis of earlier masters. 12 illustrations. 80pp. of text. 5⅜ x 8½.　　　　　　0-486-23411-8

CELTIC ART: The Methods of Construction, George Bain. Simple geometric techniques for making Celtic interlacements, spirals, Kells-type initials, animals, humans, etc. Over 500 illustrations. 160pp. 9 x 12. (Available in U.S. only.)　　　　0-486-22923-8

AN ATLAS OF ANATOMY FOR ARTISTS, Fritz Schider. Most thorough reference work on art anatomy in the world. Hundreds of illustrations, including selections from works by Vesalius, Leonardo, Goya, Ingres, Michelangelo, others. 593 illustrations. 192pp. 7⅛ x 10¼.　　　　　　　　　　　　0-486-20241-0

CELTIC HAND STROKE-BY-STROKE (Irish Half-Uncial from "The Book of Kells"): An Arthur Baker Calligraphy Manual, Arthur Baker. Complete guide to creating each letter of the alphabet in distinctive Celtic manner. Covers hand position, strokes, pens, inks, paper, more. Illustrated. 48pp. 8¼ x 11.　　　0-486-24336-2

EASY ORIGAMI, John Montroll. Charming collection of 32 projects (hat, cup, pelican, piano, swan, many more) specially designed for the novice origami hobbyist. Clearly illustrated easy-to-follow instructions insure that even beginning papercrafters will achieve successful results. 48pp. 8¼ x 11.　　　　　0-486-27298-2

BLOOMINGDALE'S ILLUSTRATED 1886 CATALOG: Fashions, Dry Goods and Housewares, Bloomingdale Brothers. Famed merchants' extremely rare catalog depicting about 1,700 products: clothing, housewares, firearms, dry goods, jewelry, more. Invaluable for dating, identifying vintage items. Also, copyright-free graphics for artists, designers. Co-published with Henry Ford Museum & Greenfield Village. 160pp. 8¼ x 11.　　　　　　　　　　　　　　0-486-25780-0

THE ART OF WORLDLY WISDOM, Baltasar Gracian. "Think with the few and speak with the many," "Friends are a second existence," and "Be able to forget" are among this 1637 volume's 300 pithy maxims. A perfect source of mental and spiritual refreshment, it can be opened at random and appreciated either in brief or at length. 128pp. 5⅜ x 8½.　　　　　　　　　　　　　0-486-44034-6

JOHNSON'S DICTIONARY: A Modern Selection, Samuel Johnson (E. L. McAdam and George Milne, eds.). This modern version reduces the original 1755 edition's 2,300 pages of definitions and literary examples to a more manageable length, retaining the verbal pleasure and historical curiosity of the original. 480pp. 5³⁄₁₆ x 8¼.　　　　　　　　　　　　　　0-486-44089-3

ADVENTURES OF HUCKLEBERRY FINN, Mark Twain, Illustrated by E. W. Kemble. A work of eternal richness and complexity, a source of ongoing critical debate, and a literary landmark, Twain's 1885 masterpiece about a barefoot boy's journey of self-discovery has enthralled readers around the world. This handsome clothbound reproduction of the first edition features all 174 of the original black-and-white illustrations. 368pp. 5⅜ x 8½.　　　　　　　　0-486-44322-1

STICKLEY CRAFTSMAN FURNITURE CATALOGS, Gustav Stickley and L. & J. G. Stickley. Beautiful, functional furniture in two authentic catalogs from 1910. 594 illustrations, including 277 photos, show settles, rockers, armchairs, reclining chairs, bookcases, desks, tables. 183pp. 6½ x 9¼. 0-486-23838-5

AMERICAN LOCOMOTIVES IN HISTORIC PHOTOGRAPHS: 1858 to 1949, Ron Ziel (ed.). A rare collection of 126 meticulously detailed official photographs, called "builder portraits," of American locomotives that majestically chronicle the rise of steam locomotive power in America. Introduction. Detailed captions. xi+ 129pp. 9 x 12. 0-486-27393-8

AMERICA'S LIGHTHOUSES: An Illustrated History, Francis Ross Holland, Jr. Delightfully written, profusely illustrated fact-filled survey of over 200 American lighthouses since 1716. History, anecdotes, technological advances, more. 240pp. 8 x 10¾. 0-486-25576-X

TOWARDS A NEW ARCHITECTURE, Le Corbusier. Pioneering manifesto by founder of "International School." Technical and aesthetic theories, views of industry, economics, relation of form to function, "mass-production split" and much more. Profusely illustrated. 320pp. 6⅛ x 9¼. (Available in U.S. only.) 0-486-25023-7

HOW THE OTHER HALF LIVES, Jacob Riis. Famous journalistic record, exposing poverty and degradation of New York slums around 1900, by major social reformer. 100 striking and influential photographs. 233pp. 10 x 7⅞. 0-486-22012-5

FRUIT KEY AND TWIG KEY TO TREES AND SHRUBS, William M. Harlow. One of the handiest and most widely used identification aids. Fruit key covers 120 deciduous and evergreen species; twig key 160 deciduous species. Easily used. Over 300 photographs. 126pp. 5⅜ x 8½. 0-486-20511-8

COMMON BIRD SONGS, Dr. Donald J. Borror. Songs of 60 most common U.S. birds: robins, sparrows, cardinals, bluejays, finches, more—arranged in order of increasing complexity. Up to 9 variations of songs of each species. Cassette and manual 0-486-99911-4

ORCHIDS AS HOUSE PLANTS, Rebecca Tyson Northen. Grow cattleyas and many other kinds of orchids—in a window, in a case, or under artificial light. 63 illustrations. 148pp. 5⅜ x 8½. 0-486-23261-1

MONSTER MAZES, Dave Phillips. Masterful mazes at four levels of difficulty. Avoid deadly perils and evil creatures to find magical treasures. Solutions for all 32 exciting illustrated puzzles. 48pp. 8¼ x 11. 0-486-26005-4

MOZART'S DON GIOVANNI (DOVER OPERA LIBRETTO SERIES), Wolfgang Amadeus Mozart. Introduced and translated by Ellen H. Bleiler. Standard Italian libretto, with complete English translation. Convenient and thoroughly portable—an ideal companion for reading along with a recording or the performance itself. Introduction. List of characters. Plot summary. 121pp. 5¼ x 8½. 0-486-24944-1

FRANK LLOYD WRIGHT'S DANA HOUSE, Donald Hoffmann. Pictorial essay of residential masterpiece with over 160 interior and exterior photos, plans, elevations, sketches and studies. 128pp. 9¼ x 10¾. 0-486-29120-0

THE CLARINET AND CLARINET PLAYING, David Pino. Lively, comprehensive work features suggestions about technique, musicianship, and musical interpretation, as well as guidelines for teaching, making your own reeds, and preparing for public performance. Includes an intriguing look at clarinet history. "A godsend," *The Clarinet,* Journal of the International Clarinet Society. Appendixes. 7 illus. 320pp. 5⅜ x 8½. 0-486-40270-3

HOLLYWOOD GLAMOR PORTRAITS, John Kobal (ed.). 145 photos from 1926-49. Harlow, Gable, Bogart, Bacall; 94 stars in all. Full background on photographers, technical aspects. 160pp. 8⅜ x 11¼. 0-486-23352-9

THE RAVEN AND OTHER FAVORITE POEMS, Edgar Allan Poe. Over 40 of the author's most memorable poems: "The Bells," "Ulalume," "Israfel," "To Helen," "The Conqueror Worm," "Eldorado," "Annabel Lee," many more. Alphabetic lists of titles and first lines. 64pp. $5\frac{3}{16}$ x 8¼. 0-486-26685-0

PERSONAL MEMOIRS OF U. S. GRANT, Ulysses Simpson Grant. Intelligent, deeply moving firsthand account of Civil War campaigns, considered by many the finest military memoirs ever written. Includes letters, historic photographs, maps and more. 528pp. 6⅛ x 9¼. 0-486-28587-1

ANCIENT EGYPTIAN MATERIALS AND INDUSTRIES, A. Lucas and J. Harris. Fascinating, comprehensive, thoroughly documented text describes this ancient civilization's vast resources and the processes that incorporated them in daily life, including the use of animal products, building materials, cosmetics, perfumes and incense, fibers, glazed ware, glass and its manufacture, materials used in the mummification process, and much more. 544pp. 6⅛ x 9¼. (Available in U.S. only.) 0-486-40446-3

RUSSIAN STORIES/RUSSKIE RASSKAZY: A Dual-Language Book, edited by Gleb Struve. Twelve tales by such masters as Chekhov, Tolstoy, Dostoevsky, Pushkin, others. Excellent word-for-word English translations on facing pages, plus teaching and study aids, Russian/English vocabulary, biographical/critical introductions, more. 416pp. 5⅜ x 8½. 0-486-26244-8

PHILADELPHIA THEN AND NOW: 60 Sites Photographed in the Past and Present, Kenneth Finkel and Susan Oyama. Rare photographs of City Hall, Logan Square, Independence Hall, Betsy Ross House, other landmarks juxtaposed with contemporary views. Captures changing face of historic city. Introduction. Captions. 128pp. 8¼ x 11. 0-486-25790-8

NORTH AMERICAN INDIAN LIFE: Customs and Traditions of 23 Tribes, Elsie Clews Parsons (ed.). 27 fictionalized essays by noted anthropologists examine religion, customs, government, additional facets of life among the Winnebago, Crow, Zuni, Eskimo, other tribes. 480pp. 6⅛ x 9¼. 0-486-27377-6

TECHNICAL MANUAL AND DICTIONARY OF CLASSICAL BALLET, Gail Grant. Defines, explains, comments on steps, movements, poses and concepts. 15-page pictorial section. Basic book for student, viewer. 127pp. 5⅜ x 8½. 0-486-21843-0

THE MALE AND FEMALE FIGURE IN MOTION: 60 Classic Photographic Sequences, Eadweard Muybridge. 60 true-action photographs of men and women walking, running, climbing, bending, turning, etc., reproduced from rare 19th-century masterpiece. vi + 121pp. 9 x 12. 0-486-24745-7

CATALOG OF DOVER BOOKS

ANIMALS: 1,419 Copyright-Free Illustrations of Mammals, Birds, Fish, Insects, etc., Jim Harter (ed.). Clear wood engravings present, in extremely lifelike poses, over 1,000 species of animals. One of the most extensive pictorial sourcebooks of its kind. Captions. Index. 284pp. 9 x 12. 0-486-23766-4

1001 QUESTIONS ANSWERED ABOUT THE SEASHORE, N. J. Berrill and Jacquelyn Berrill. Queries answered about dolphins, sea snails, sponges, starfish, fishes, shore birds, many others. Covers appearance, breeding, growth, feeding, much more. 305pp. 5¼ x 8¼. 0-486-23366-9

ATTRACTING BIRDS TO YOUR YARD, William J. Weber. Easy-to-follow guide offers advice on how to attract the greatest diversity of birds: birdhouses, feeders, water and waterers, much more. 96pp. 5³⁄₁₆ x 8¼. 0-486-28927-3

MEDICINAL AND OTHER USES OF NORTH AMERICAN PLANTS: A Historical Survey with Special Reference to the Eastern Indian Tribes, Charlotte Erichsen-Brown. Chronological historical citations document 500 years of usage of plants, trees, shrubs native to eastern Canada, northeastern U.S. Also complete identifying information. 343 illustrations. 544pp. 6½ x 9¼. 0-486-25951-X

STORYBOOK MAZES, Dave Phillips. 23 stories and mazes on two-page spreads: Wizard of Oz, Treasure Island, Robin Hood, etc. Solutions. 64pp. 8¼ x 11.
0-486-23628-5

AMERICAN NEGRO SONGS: 230 Folk Songs and Spirituals, Religious and Secular, John W. Work. This authoritative study traces the African influences of songs sung and played by black Americans at work, in church, and as entertainment. The author discusses the lyric significance of such songs as "Swing Low, Sweet Chariot," "John Henry," and others and offers the words and music for 230 songs. Bibliography. Index of Song Titles. 272pp. 6½ x 9¼. 0-486-40271-1

MOVIE-STAR PORTRAITS OF THE FORTIES, John Kobal (ed.). 163 glamor, studio photos of 106 stars of the 1940s: Rita Hayworth, Ava Gardner, Marlon Brando, Clark Gable, many more. 176pp. 8⅜ x 11¼. 0-486-23546-7

YEKL and THE IMPORTED BRIDEGROOM AND OTHER STORIES OF YIDDISH NEW YORK, Abraham Cahan. Film Hester Street based on *Yekl* (1896). Novel, other stories among first about Jewish immigrants on N.Y.'s East Side. 240pp. 5⅜ x 8½. 0-486-22427-9

SELECTED POEMS, Walt Whitman. Generous sampling from *Leaves of Grass*. Twenty-four poems include "I Hear America Singing," "Song of the Open Road," "I Sing the Body Electric," "When Lilacs Last in the Dooryard Bloom'd," "O Captain! My Captain!"—all reprinted from an authoritative edition. Lists of titles and first lines. 128pp. 5³⁄₁₆ x 8¼. 0-486-26878-0

SONGS OF EXPERIENCE: Facsimile Reproduction with 26 Plates in Full Color, William Blake. 26 full-color plates from a rare 1826 edition. Includes "The Tyger," "London," "Holy Thursday," and other poems. Printed text of poems. 48pp. 5¼ x 7.
0-486-24636-1

THE BEST TALES OF HOFFMANN, E. T. A. Hoffmann. 10 of Hoffmann's most important stories: "Nutcracker and the King of Mice," "The Golden Flowerpot," etc. 458pp. 5⅜ x 8½. 0-486-21793-0

THE BOOK OF TEA, Kakuzo Okakura. Minor classic of the Orient: entertaining, charming explanation, interpretation of traditional Japanese culture in terms of tea ceremony. 94pp. 5⅜ x 8½. 0-486-20070-1

CATALOG OF DOVER BOOKS

FRENCH STORIES/CONTES FRANÇAIS: A Dual-Language Book, Wallace Fowlie. Ten stories by French masters, Voltaire to Camus: "Micromegas" by Voltaire; "The Atheist's Mass" by Balzac; "Minuet" by de Maupassant; "The Guest" by Camus, six more. Excellent English translations on facing pages. Also French-English vocabulary list, exercises, more. 352pp. 5⅜ x 8½. 0-486-26443-2

CHICAGO AT THE TURN OF THE CENTURY IN PHOTOGRAPHS: 122 Historic Views from the Collections of the Chicago Historical Society, Larry A. Viskochil. Rare large-format prints offer detailed views of City Hall, State Street, the Loop, Hull House, Union Station, many other landmarks, circa 1904-1913. Introduction. Captions. Maps. 144pp. 9⅜ x 12¼. 0-486-24656-6

OLD BROOKLYN IN EARLY PHOTOGRAPHS, 1865-1929, William Lee Younger. Luna Park, Gravesend race track, construction of Grand Army Plaza, moving of Hotel Brighton, etc. 157 previously unpublished photographs. 165pp. 8⅞ x 11¾. 0-486-23587-4

THE MYTHS OF THE NORTH AMERICAN INDIANS, Lewis Spence. Rich anthology of the myths and legends of the Algonquins, Iroquois, Pawnees and Sioux, prefaced by an extensive historical and ethnological commentary. 36 illustrations. 480pp. 5⅜ x 8½. 0-486-25967-6

AN ENCYCLOPEDIA OF BATTLES: Accounts of Over 1,560 Battles from 1479 B.C. to the Present, David Eggenberger. Essential details of every major battle in recorded history from the first battle of Megiddo in 1479 B.C. to Grenada in 1984. List of Battle Maps. New Appendix covering the years 1967-1984. Index. 99 illustrations. 544pp. 6½ x 9¼. 0-486-24913-1

SAILING ALONE AROUND THE WORLD, Captain Joshua Slocum. First man to sail around the world, alone, in small boat. One of great feats of seamanship told in delightful manner. 67 illustrations. 294pp. 5⅜ x 8½. 0-486-20326-3

ANARCHISM AND OTHER ESSAYS, Emma Goldman. Powerful, penetrating, prophetic essays on direct action, role of minorities, prison reform, puritan hypocrisy, violence, etc. 271pp. 5⅜ x 8½. 0-486-22484-8

MYTHS OF THE HINDUS AND BUDDHISTS, Ananda K. Coomaraswamy and Sister Nivedita. Great stories of the epics; deeds of Krishna, Shiva, taken from puranas, Vedas, folk tales; etc. 32 illustrations. 400pp. 5⅜ x 8½. 0-486-21759-0

MY BONDAGE AND MY FREEDOM, Frederick Douglass. Born a slave, Douglass became outspoken force in antislavery movement. The best of Douglass' autobiographies. Graphic description of slave life. 464pp. 5⅜ x 8½. 0-486-22457-0

FOLLOWING THE EQUATOR: A Journey Around the World, Mark Twain. Fascinating humorous account of 1897 voyage to Hawaii, Australia, India, New Zealand, etc. Ironic, bemused reports on peoples, customs, climate, flora and fauna, politics, much more. 197 illustrations. 720pp. 5⅜ x 8½. 0-486-26113-1

THE PEOPLE CALLED SHAKERS, Edward D. Andrews. Definitive study of Shakers: origins, beliefs, practices, dances, social organization, furniture and crafts, etc. 33 illustrations. 351pp. 5⅜ x 8½. 0-486-21081-2

THE MYTHS OF GREECE AND ROME, H. A. Guerber. A classic of mythology, generously illustrated, long prized for its simple, graphic, accurate retelling of the principal myths of Greece and Rome, and for its commentary on their origins and significance. With 64 illustrations by Michelangelo, Raphael, Titian, Rubens, Canova, Bernini and others. 480pp. 5⅜ x 8½. 0-486-27584-1

PSYCHOLOGY OF MUSIC, Carl E. Seashore. Classic work discusses music as a medium from psychological viewpoint. Clear treatment of physical acoustics, auditory apparatus, sound perception, development of musical skills, nature of musical feeling, host of other topics. 88 figures. 408pp. 5⅜ x 8½. 0-486-21851-1

LIFE IN ANCIENT EGYPT, Adolf Erman. Fullest, most thorough, detailed older account with much not in more recent books, domestic life, religion, magic, medicine, commerce, much more. Many illustrations reproduce tomb paintings, carvings, hieroglyphs, etc. 597pp. 5⅜ x 8½. 0-486-22632-8

SUNDIALS, Their Theory and Construction, Albert Waugh. Far and away the best, most thorough coverage of ideas, mathematics concerned, types, construction, adjusting anywhere. Simple, nontechnical treatment allows even children to build several of these dials. Over 100 illustrations. 230pp. 5⅜ x 8½. 0-486-22947-5

THEORETICAL HYDRODYNAMICS, L. M. Milne-Thomson. Classic exposition of the mathematical theory of fluid motion, applicable to both hydrodynamics and aerodynamics. Over 600 exercises. 768pp. 6⅛ x 9¼. 0-486-68970-0

OLD-TIME VIGNETTES IN FULL COLOR, Carol Belanger Grafton (ed.). Over 390 charming, often sentimental illustrations, selected from archives of Victorian graphics–pretty women posing, children playing, food, flowers, kittens and puppies, smiling cherubs, birds and butterflies, much more. All copyright-free. 48pp. 9¼ x 12¼. 0-486-27269-9

PERSPECTIVE FOR ARTISTS, Rex Vicat Cole. Depth, perspective of sky and sea, shadows, much more, not usually covered. 391 diagrams, 81 reproductions of drawings and paintings. 279pp. 5⅜ x 8½. 0-486-22487-2

DRAWING THE LIVING FIGURE, Joseph Sheppard. Innovative approach to artistic anatomy focuses on specifics of surface anatomy, rather than muscles and bones. Over 170 drawings of live models in front, back and side views, and in widely varying poses. Accompanying diagrams. 177 illustrations. Introduction. Index. 144pp. 8⅜ x11¼. 0-486-26723-7

GOTHIC AND OLD ENGLISH ALPHABETS: 100 Complete Fonts, Dan X. Solo. Add power, elegance to posters, signs, other graphics with 100 stunning copyright-free alphabets: Blackstone, Dolbey, Germania, 97 more–including many lower-case, numerals, punctuation marks. 104pp. 8⅛ x 11. 0-486-24695-7

THE BOOK OF WOOD CARVING, Charles Marshall Sayers. Finest book for beginners discusses fundamentals and offers 34 designs. "Absolutely first rate . . . well thought out and well executed."–E. J. Tangerman. 118pp. 7¾ x 10⅝. 0-486-23654-4

ILLUSTRATED CATALOG OF CIVIL WAR MILITARY GOODS: Union Army Weapons, Insignia, Uniform Accessories, and Other Equipment, Schuyler, Hartley, and Graham. Rare, profusely illustrated 1846 catalog includes Union Army uniform and dress regulations, arms and ammunition, coats, insignia, flags, swords, rifles, etc. 226 illustrations. 160pp. 9 x 12. 0-486-24939-5

WOMEN'S FASHIONS OF THE EARLY 1900s: An Unabridged Republication of "New York Fashions, 1909," National Cloak & Suit Co. Rare catalog of mail-order fashions documents women's and children's clothing styles shortly after the turn of the century. Captions offer full descriptions, prices. Invaluable resource for fashion, costume historians. Approximately 725 illustrations. 128pp. 8⅜ x 11¼. 0-486-27276-1

HOW TO DO BEADWORK, Mary White. Fundamental book on craft from simple projects to five-bead chains and woven works. 106 illustrations. 142pp. 5⅜ x 8.
0-486-20697-1

THE 1912 AND 1915 GUSTAV STICKLEY FURNITURE CATALOGS, Gustav Stickley. With over 200 detailed illustrations and descriptions, these two catalogs are essential reading and reference materials and identification guides for Stickley furniture. Captions cite materials, dimensions and prices. 112pp. 6½ x 9¼. 0-486-26676-1

EARLY AMERICAN LOCOMOTIVES, John H. White, Jr. Finest locomotive engravings from early 19th century: historical (1804–74), main-line (after 1870), special, foreign, etc. 147 plates. 142pp. 11⅜ x 8¼.
0-486-22772-3

LITTLE BOOK OF EARLY AMERICAN CRAFTS AND TRADES, Peter Stockham (ed.). 1807 children's book explains crafts and trades: baker, hatter, cooper, potter, and many others. 23 copperplate illustrations. 140pp. 4⁵/₈ x 6.
0-486-23336-7

VICTORIAN FASHIONS AND COSTUMES FROM HARPER'S BAZAR, 1867–1898, Stella Blum (ed.). Day costumes, evening wear, sports clothes, shoes, hats, other accessories in over 1,000 detailed engravings. 320pp. 9⅜ x 12¼.
0-486-22990-4

THE LONG ISLAND RAIL ROAD IN EARLY PHOTOGRAPHS, Ron Ziel. Over 220 rare photos, informative text document origin (1844) and development of rail service on Long Island. Vintage views of early trains, locomotives, stations, passengers, crews, much more. Captions. 8⅞ x 11¾. 0-486-26301-0

VOYAGE OF THE LIBERDADE, Joshua Slocum. Great 19th-century mariner's thrilling, first-hand account of the wreck of his ship off South America, the 35-foot boat he built from the wreckage, and its remarkable voyage home. 128pp. 5⅜ x 8½.
0-486-40022-0

TEN BOOKS ON ARCHITECTURE, Vitruvius. The most important book ever written on architecture. Early Roman aesthetics, technology, classical orders, site selection, all other aspects. Morgan translation. 331pp. 5⅜ x 8½. 0-486-20645-9

THE HUMAN FIGURE IN MOTION, Eadweard Muybridge. More than 4,500 stopped-action photos, in action series, showing undraped men, women, children jumping, lying down, throwing, sitting, wrestling, carrying, etc. 390pp. 7⅞ x 10⅝.
0-486-20204-6 Clothbd.

TREES OF THE EASTERN AND CENTRAL UNITED STATES AND CANADA, William M. Harlow. Best one-volume guide to 140 trees. Full descriptions, woodlore, range, etc. Over 600 illustrations. Handy size. 288pp. 4½ x 6⅜. 0-486-20395-6

GROWING AND USING HERBS AND SPICES, Milo Miloradovich. Versatile handbook provides all the information needed for cultivation and use of all the herbs and spices available in North America. 4 illustrations. Index. Glossary. 236pp. 5⅜ x 8½.
0-486-25058-X

BIG BOOK OF MAZES AND LABYRINTHS, Walter Shepherd. 50 mazes and labyrinths in all–classical, solid, ripple, and more–in one great volume. Perfect inexpensive puzzler for clever youngsters. Full solutions. 112pp. 8⅛ x 11. 0-486-22951-3

PIANO TUNING, J. Cree Fischer. Clearest, best book for beginner, amateur. Simple repairs, raising dropped notes, tuning by easy method of flattened fifths. No previous skills needed. 4 illustrations. 201pp. 5⅜ x 8½. 0-486-23267-0

CATALOG OF DOVER BOOKS

HINTS TO SINGERS; Lillian Nordica. Selecting the right teacher, developing confidence, overcoming stage fright, and many other important skills receive thoughtful discussion in this indispensible guide, written by a world-famous diva of four decades' experience. 96pp. 5⅜ x 8½. 0-486-40094-8

THE COMPLETE NONSENSE OF EDWARD LEAR, Edward Lear. All nonsense limericks, zany alphabets, Owl and Pussycat, songs, nonsense botany, etc., illustrated by Lear. Total of 320pp. 5⅜ x 8½. (Available in U.S. only.) 0-486-20167-8

VICTORIAN PARLOUR POETRY: An Annotated Anthology, Michael R. Turner. 117 gems by Longfellow, Tennyson, Browning, many lesser-known poets. "The Village Blacksmith," "Curfew Must Not Ring Tonight," "Only a Baby Small," dozens more, often difficult to find elsewhere. Index of poets, titles, first lines. xxiii + 325pp. 5⅜ x 8¼. 0-486-27044-0

DUBLINERS, James Joyce. Fifteen stories offer vivid, tightly focused observations of the lives of Dublin's poorer classes. At least one, "The Dead," is considered a masterpiece. Reprinted complete and unabridged from standard edition. 160pp. 5³⁄₁₆ x 8¼. 0-486-26870-5

GREAT WEIRD TALES: 14 Stories by Lovecraft, Blackwood, Machen and Others, S. T. Joshi (ed.). 14 spellbinding tales, including "The Sin Eater," by Fiona McLeod, "The Eye Above the Mantel," by Frank Belknap Long, as well as renowned works by R. H. Barlow, Lord Dunsany, Arthur Machen, W. C. Morrow and eight other masters of the genre. 256pp. 5⅜ x 8½. (Available in U.S. only.) 0-486-40436-6

THE BOOK OF THE SACRED MAGIC OF ABRAMELIN THE MAGE, translated by S. MacGregor Mathers. Medieval manuscript of ceremonial magic. Basic document in Aleister Crowley, Golden Dawn groups. 268pp. 5⅜ x 8½. 0-486-23211-5

THE BATTLES THAT CHANGED HISTORY, Fletcher Pratt. Eminent historian profiles 16 crucial conflicts, ancient to modern, that changed the course of civilization. 352pp. 5⅜ x 8½. 0-486-41129-X

NEW RUSSIAN-ENGLISH AND ENGLISH-RUSSIAN DICTIONARY, M. A. O'Brien. This is a remarkably handy Russian dictionary, containing a surprising amount of information, including over 70,000 entries. 366pp. 4½ x 6⅛. 0-486-20208-9

NEW YORK IN THE FORTIES, Andreas Feininger. 162 brilliant photographs by the well-known photographer, formerly with *Life* magazine. Commuters, shoppers, Times Square at night, much else from city at its peak. Captions by John von Hartz. 181pp. 9¼ x 10¾. 0-486-23585-8

INDIAN SIGN LANGUAGE, William Tomkins. Over 525 signs developed by Sioux and other tribes. Written instructions and diagrams. Also 290 pictographs. 111pp. 6⅛ x 9¼. 0-486-22029-X

ANATOMY: A Complete Guide for Artists, Joseph Sheppard. A master of figure drawing shows artists how to render human anatomy convincingly. Over 460 illustrations. 224pp. 8⅜ x 11¼. 0-486-27279-6

MEDIEVAL CALLIGRAPHY: Its History and Technique, Marc Drogin. Spirited history, comprehensive instruction manual covers 13 styles (ca. 4th century through 15th). Excellent photographs; directions for duplicating medieval techniques with modern tools. 224pp. 8⅜ x 11¼. 0-486-26142-5

DRIED FLOWERS: How to Prepare Them, Sarah Whitlock and Martha Rankin. Complete instructions on how to use silica gel, meal and borax, perlite aggregate, sand and borax, glycerine and water to create attractive permanent flower arrangements. 12 illustrations. 32pp. 5⅜ x 8½. 0-486-21802-3

EASY-TO-MAKE BIRD FEEDERS FOR WOODWORKERS, Scott D. Campbell. Detailed, simple-to-use guide for designing, constructing, caring for and using feeders. Text, illustrations for 12 classic and contemporary designs. 96pp. 5⅜ x 8½. 0-486-25847-5

THE COMPLETE BOOK OF BIRDHOUSE CONSTRUCTION FOR WOOD-WORKERS, Scott D. Campbell. Detailed instructions, illustrations, tables. Also data on bird habitat and instinct patterns. Bibliography. 3 tables. 63 illustrations in 15 figures. 48pp. 5¼ x 8½. 0-486-24407-5

SCOTTISH WONDER TALES FROM MYTH AND LEGEND, Donald A. Mackenzie. 16 lively tales tell of giants rumbling down mountainsides, of a magic wand that turns stone pillars into warriors, of gods and goddesses, evil hags, powerful forces and more. 240pp. 5⅜ x 8½. 0-486-29677-6

THE HISTORY OF UNDERCLOTHES, C. Willett Cunnington and Phyllis Cunnington. Fascinating, well-documented survey covering six centuries of English undergarments, enhanced with over 100 illustrations: 12th-century laced-up bodice, footed long drawers (1795), 19th-century bustles, l9th-century corsets for men, Victorian "bust improvers," much more. 272pp. 5⅜ x 8¼. 0-486-27124-2

ARTS AND CRAFTS FURNITURE: The Complete Brooks Catalog of 1912, Brooks Manufacturing Co. Photos and detailed descriptions of more than 150 now very collectible furniture designs from the Arts and Crafts movement depict davenports, settees, buffets, desks, tables, chairs, bedsteads, dressers and more, all built of solid, quarter-sawed oak. Invaluable for students and enthusiasts of antiques, Americana and the decorative arts. 80pp. 6½ x 9¼. 0-486-27471-3

WILBUR AND ORVILLE: A Biography of the Wright Brothers, Fred Howard. Definitive, crisply written study tells the full story of the brothers' lives and work. A vividly written biography, unparalleled in scope and color, that also captures the spirit of an extraordinary era. 560pp. 6⅛ x 9¼. 0-486-40297-5

THE ARTS OF THE SAILOR: Knotting, Splicing and Ropework, Hervey Garrett Smith. Indispensable shipboard reference covers tools, basic knots and useful hitches; handsewing and canvas work, more. Over 100 illustrations. Delightful reading for sea lovers. 256pp. 5⅜ x 8½. 0-486-26440-8

FRANK LLOYD WRIGHT'S FALLINGWATER: The House and Its History, Second, Revised Edition, Donald Hoffmann. A total revision—both in text and illustrations—of the standard document on Fallingwater, the boldest, most personal architectural statement of Wright's mature years, updated with valuable new material from the recently opened Frank Lloyd Wright Archives. "Fascinating"—*The New York Times*. 116 illustrations. 128pp. 9¼ x 10¾. 0-486-27430-6

PHOTOGRAPHIC SKETCHBOOK OF THE CIVIL WAR, Alexander Gardner. 100 photos taken on field during the Civil War. Famous shots of Manassas Harper's Ferry, Lincoln, Richmond, slave pens, etc. 244pp. 10⅝ x 8¼. 0-486-22731-6

FIVE ACRES AND INDEPENDENCE, Maurice G. Kains. Great back-to-the-land classic explains basics of self-sufficient farming. The one book to get. 95 illustrations. 397pp. 5⅜ x 8½. 0-486-20974-1

CATALOG OF DOVER BOOKS

A MODERN HERBAL, Margaret Grieve. Much the fullest, most exact, most useful compilation of herbal material. Gigantic alphabetical encyclopedia, from aconite to zedoary, gives botanical information, medical properties, folklore, economic uses, much else. Indispensable to serious reader. 161 illustrations. 888pp. 6½ x 9¼. 2-vol. set. (Available in U.S. only.)   Vol. I: 0-486-22798-7   Vol. II: 0-486-22799-5

HIDDEN TREASURE MAZE BOOK, Dave Phillips. Solve 34 challenging mazes accompanied by heroic tales of adventure. Evil dragons, people-eating plants, blood-thirsty giants, many more dangerous adversaries lurk at every twist and turn. 34 mazes, stories, solutions. 48pp. 8¼ x 11.   0-486-24566-7

LETTERS OF W. A. MOZART, Wolfgang A. Mozart. Remarkable letters show bawdy wit, humor, imagination, musical insights, contemporary musical world; includes some letters from Leopold Mozart. 276pp. 5⅜ x 8½.   0-486-22859-2

BASIC PRINCIPLES OF CLASSICAL BALLET, Agrippina Vaganova. Great Russian theoretician, teacher explains methods for teaching classical ballet. 118 illustrations. 175pp. 5⅜ x 8½.   0-486-22036-2

THE JUMPING FROG, Mark Twain. Revenge edition. The original story of The Celebrated Jumping Frog of Calaveras County, a hapless French translation, and Twain's hilarious "retranslation" from the French. 12 illustrations. 66pp. 5⅜ x 8½.
0-486-22686-7

BEST REMEMBERED POEMS, Martin Gardner (ed.). The 126 poems in this superb collection of 19th- and 20th-century British and American verse range from Shelley's "To a Skylark" to the impassioned "Renascence" of Edna St. Vincent Millay and to Edward Lear's whimsical "The Owl and the Pussycat." 224pp. 5⅜ x 8½.
0-486-27165-X

COMPLETE SONNETS, William Shakespeare. Over 150 exquisite poems deal with love, friendship, the tyranny of time, beauty's evanescence, death and other themes in language of remarkable power, precision and beauty. Glossary of archaic terms. 80pp. 5³⁄₁₆ x 8¼.   0-486-26686-9

HISTORIC HOMES OF THE AMERICAN PRESIDENTS, Second, Revised Edition, Irvin Haas. A traveler's guide to American Presidential homes, most open to the public, depicting and describing homes occupied by every American President from George Washington to George Bush. With visiting hours, admission charges, travel routes. 175 photographs. Index. 160pp. 8¼ x 11.   0-486-26751-2

THE WIT AND HUMOR OF OSCAR WILDE, Alvin Redman (ed.). More than 1,000 ripostes, paradoxes, wisecracks: Work is the curse of the drinking classes; I can resist everything except temptation; etc. 258pp. 5⅜ x 8½.   0-486-20602-5

SHAKESPEARE LEXICON AND QUOTATION DICTIONARY, Alexander Schmidt. Full definitions, locations, shades of meaning in every word in plays and poems. More than 50,000 exact quotations. 1,485pp. 6½ x 9¼. 2-vol. set.
Vol. 1: 0-486-22726-X   Vol. 2: 0-486-22727-8

SELECTED POEMS, Emily Dickinson. Over 100 best-known, best-loved poems by one of America's foremost poets, reprinted from authoritative early editions. No comparable edition at this price. Index of first lines. 64pp. 5³⁄₁₆ x 8¼. 0-486-26466-1

THE INSIDIOUS DR. FU-MANCHU, Sax Rohmer. The first of the popular mystery series introduces a pair of English detectives to their archnemesis, the diabolical Dr. Fu-Manchu. Flavorful atmosphere, fast-paced action, and colorful characters enliven this classic of the genre. 208pp. 5³⁄₁₆ x 8¼.   0-486-29898-1

CATALOG OF DOVER BOOKS

THE MALLEUS MALEFICARUM OF KRAMER AND SPRENGER, translated by Montague Summers. Full text of most important witchhunter's "bible," used by both Catholics and Protestants. 278pp. 6⅝ x 10. 0-486-22802-9

SPANISH STORIES/CUENTOS ESPAÑOLES: A Dual-Language Book, Angel Flores (ed.). Unique format offers 13 great stories in Spanish by Cervantes, Borges, others. Faithful English translations on facing pages. 352pp. 5⅜ x 8½.
0-486-25399-6

GARDEN CITY, LONG ISLAND, IN EARLY PHOTOGRAPHS, 1869–1919, Mildred H. Smith. Handsome treasury of 118 vintage pictures, accompanied by carefully researched captions, document the Garden City Hotel fire (1899), the Vanderbilt Cup Race (1908), the first airmail flight departing from the Nassau Boulevard Aerodrome (1911), and much more. 96pp. 8⅞ x 11¾. 0-486-40669-5

OLD QUEENS, N.Y., IN EARLY PHOTOGRAPHS, Vincent F. Seyfried and William Asadorian. Over 160 rare photographs of Maspeth, Jamaica, Jackson Heights, and other areas. Vintage views of DeWitt Clinton mansion, 1939 World's Fair and more. Captions. 192pp. 8⅞ x 11. 0-486-26358-4

CAPTURED BY THE INDIANS: 15 Firsthand Accounts, 1750-1870, Frederick Drimmer. Astounding true historical accounts of grisly torture, bloody conflicts, relentless pursuits, miraculous escapes and more, by people who lived to tell the tale. 384pp. 5⅜ x 8½. 0-486-24901-8

THE WORLD'S GREAT SPEECHES (Fourth Enlarged Edition), Lewis Copeland, Lawrence W. Lamm, and Stephen J. McKenna. Nearly 300 speeches provide public speakers with a wealth of updated quotes and inspiration–from Pericles' funeral oration and William Jennings Bryan's "Cross of Gold Speech" to Malcolm X's powerful words on the Black Revolution and Earl of Spenser's tribute to his sister, Diana, Princess of Wales. 944pp. 5⅜ x 8⅜. 0-486-40903-1

THE BOOK OF THE SWORD, Sir Richard F. Burton. Great Victorian scholar/adventurer's eloquent, erudite history of the "queen of weapons"–from prehistory to early Roman Empire. Evolution and development of early swords, variations (sabre, broadsword, cutlass, scimitar, etc.), much more. 336pp. 6⅛ x 9¼.
0-486-25434-8

AUTOBIOGRAPHY: The Story of My Experiments with Truth, Mohandas K. Gandhi. Boyhood, legal studies, purification, the growth of the Satyagraha (nonviolent protest) movement. Critical, inspiring work of the man responsible for the freedom of India. 480pp. 5⅜ x 8½. (Available in U.S. only.) 0-486-24593-4

CELTIC MYTHS AND LEGENDS, T. W. Rolleston. Masterful retelling of Irish and Welsh stories and tales. Cuchulain, King Arthur, Deirdre, the Grail, many more. First paperback edition. 58 full-page illustrations. 512pp. 5⅜ x 8½. 0-486-26507-2

THE PRINCIPLES OF PSYCHOLOGY, William James. Famous long course complete, unabridged. Stream of thought, time perception, memory, experimental methods; great work decades ahead of its time. 94 figures. 1,391pp. 5⅜ x 8½. 2-vol. set.
Vol. I: 0-486-20381-6   Vol. II: 0-486-20382-4

THE WORLD AS WILL AND REPRESENTATION, Arthur Schopenhauer. Definitive English translation of Schopenhauer's life work, correcting more than 1,000 errors, omissions in earlier translations. Translated by E. F. J. Payne. Total of 1,269pp. 5⅜ x 8½. 2-vol. set.   Vol. 1: 0-486-21761-2   Vol. 2: 0-486-21762-0

CATALOG OF DOVER BOOKS

MAGIC AND MYSTERY IN TIBET, Madame Alexandra David-Neel. Experiences among lamas, magicians, sages, sorcerers, Bonpa wizards. A true psychic discovery. 32 illustrations. 321pp. 5⅜ x 8½. (Available in U.S. only.)   0-486-22682-4

THE EGYPTIAN BOOK OF THE DEAD, E. A. Wallis Budge. Complete reproduction of Ani's papyrus, finest ever found. Full hieroglyphic text, interlinear transliteration, word-for-word translation, smooth translation. 533pp. 6½ x 9¼.

0-486-21866-X

HISTORIC COSTUME IN PICTURES, Braun & Schneider. Over 1,450 costumed figures in clearly detailed engravings–from dawn of civilization to end of 19th century. Captions. Many folk costumes. 256pp. 8⅜ x 11¾.   0-486-23150-X

MATHEMATICS FOR THE NONMATHEMATICIAN, Morris Kline. Detailed, college-level treatment of mathematics in cultural and historical context, with numerous exercises. Recommended Reading Lists. Tables. Numerous figures. 641pp. 5⅜ x 8½.

0-486-24823-2

PROBABILISTIC METHODS IN THE THEORY OF STRUCTURES, Isaac Elishakoff. Well-written introduction covers the elements of the theory of probability from two or more random variables, the reliability of such multivariable structures, the theory of random function, Monte Carlo methods of treating problems incapable of exact solution, and more. Examples. 502pp. 5⅜ x 8½.   0-486-40691-1

THE RIME OF THE ANCIENT MARINER, Gustave Doré, S. T. Coleridge. Doré's finest work; 34 plates capture moods, subtleties of poem. Flawless full-size reproductions printed on facing pages with authoritative text of poem. "Beautiful. Simply beautiful."–*Publisher's Weekly.* 77pp. 9¼ x 12.   0-486-22305-1

SCULPTURE: Principles and Practice, Louis Slobodkin. Step-by-step approach to clay, plaster, metals, stone; classical and modern. 253 drawings, photos. 255pp. 8⅛ x 11.

0-486-22960-2

THE INFLUENCE OF SEA POWER UPON HISTORY, 1660–1783, A. T. Mahan. Influential classic of naval history and tactics still used as text in war colleges. First paperback edition. 4 maps. 24 battle plans. 640pp. 5⅜ x 8½.   0-486-25509-3

THE STORY OF THE TITANIC AS TOLD BY ITS SURVIVORS, Jack Winocour (ed.). What it was really like. Panic, despair, shocking inefficiency, and a little heroism. More thrilling than any fictional account. 26 illustrations. 320pp. 5⅜ x 8½.

0-486-20610-6

ONE TWO THREE . . . INFINITY: Facts and Speculations of Science, George Gamow. Great physicist's fascinating, readable overview of contemporary science: number theory, relativity, fourth dimension, entropy, genes, atomic structure, much more. 128 illustrations. Index. 352pp. 5⅜ x 8½.   0-486-25664-2

DALÍ ON MODERN ART: The Cuckolds of Antiquated Modern Art, Salvador Dalí. Influential painter skewers modern art and its practitioners. Outrageous evaluations of Picasso, Cézanne, Turner, more. 15 renderings of paintings discussed. 44 calligraphic decorations by Dalí. 96pp. 5⅜ x 8½. (Available in U.S. only.)   0-486-29220-7

ANTIQUE PLAYING CARDS: A Pictorial History, Henry René D'Allemagne. Over 900 elaborate, decorative images from rare playing cards (14th–20th centuries): Bacchus, death, dancing dogs, hunting scenes, royal coats of arms, players cheating, much more. 96pp. 9¼ x 12¼.   0-486-29265-7

MAKING FURNITURE MASTERPIECES: 30 Projects with Measured Drawings, Franklin H. Gottshall. Step-by-step instructions, illustrations for constructing handsome, useful pieces, among them a Sheraton desk, Chippendale chair, Spanish desk, Queen Anne table and a William and Mary dressing mirror. 224pp. 8⅛ x 11¼. 0-486-29338-6

NORTH AMERICAN INDIAN DESIGNS FOR ARTISTS AND CRAFTSPEOPLE, Eva Wilson. Over 360 authentic copyright-free designs adapted from Navajo blankets, Hopi pottery, Sioux buffalo hides, more. Geometrics, symbolic figures, plant and animal motifs, etc. 128pp. 8⅜ x 11. (Not for sale in the United Kingdom.) 0-486-25341-4

THE FOSSIL BOOK: A Record of Prehistoric Life, Patricia V. Rich et al. Profusely illustrated definitive guide covers everything from single-celled organisms and dinosaurs to birds and mammals and the interplay between climate and man. Over 1,500 illustrations. 760pp. 7½ x 10⅛. 0-486-29371-8

VICTORIAN ARCHITECTURAL DETAILS: Designs for Over 700 Stairs, Mantels, Doors, Windows, Cornices, Porches, and Other Decorative Elements, A. J. Bicknell & Company. Everything from dormer windows and piazzas to balconies and gable ornaments. Also includes elevations and floor plans for handsome, private residences and commercial structures. 80pp. 9⅜ x 12¼. 0-486-44015-X

WESTERN ISLAMIC ARCHITECTURE: A Concise Introduction, John D. Hoag. Profusely illustrated critical appraisal compares and contrasts Islamic mosques and palaces–from Spain and Egypt to other areas in the Middle East. 139 illustrations. 128pp. 6 x 9. 0-486-43760-4

CHINESE ARCHITECTURE: A Pictorial History, Liang Ssu-ch'eng. More than 240 rare photographs and drawings depict temples, pagodas, tombs, bridges, and imperial palaces comprising much of China's architectural heritage. 152 halftones, 94 diagrams. 232pp. 10¾ x 9⅞. 0-486-43999-2

THE RENAISSANCE: Studies in Art and Poetry, Walter Pater. One of the most talked-about books of the 19th century, *The Renaissance* combines scholarship and philosophy in an innovative work of cultural criticism that examines the achievements of Botticelli, Leonardo, Michelangelo, and other artists. "The holy writ of beauty."–Oscar Wilde. 160pp. 5⅜ x 8½. 0-486-44025-7

A TREATISE ON PAINTING, Leonardo da Vinci. The great Renaissance artist's practical advice on drawing and painting techniques covers anatomy, perspective, composition, light and shadow, and color. A classic of art instruction, it features 48 drawings by Nicholas Poussin and Leon Battista Alberti. 192pp. 5⅜ x 8½. 0-486-44155-5

THE MIND OF LEONARDO DA VINCI, Edward McCurdy. More than just a biography, this classic study by a distinguished historian draws upon Leonardo's extensive writings to offer numerous demonstrations of the Renaissance master's achievements, not only in sculpture and painting, but also in music, engineering, and even experimental aviation. 384pp. 5⅜ x 8½. 0-486-44142-3

WASHINGTON IRVING'S RIP VAN WINKLE, Illustrated by Arthur Rackham. Lovely prints that established artist as a leading illustrator of the time and forever etched into the popular imagination a classic of Catskill lore. 51 full-color plates. 80pp. 8⅜ x 11. 0-486-44242-X

HENSCHE ON PAINTING, John W. Robichaux. Basic painting philosophy and methodology of a great teacher, as expounded in his famous classes and workshops on Cape Cod. 7 illustrations in color on covers. 80pp. 5⅜ x 8½. 0-486-43728-0

LIGHT AND SHADE: A Classic Approach to Three-Dimensional Drawing, Mrs. Mary P. Merrifield. Handy reference clearly demonstrates principles of light and shade by revealing effects of common daylight, sunshine, and candle or artificial light on geometrical solids. 13 plates. 64pp. 5⅜ x 8½. 0-486-44143-1

ASTROLOGY AND ASTRONOMY: A Pictorial Archive of Signs and Symbols, Ernst and Johanna Lehner. Treasure trove of stories, lore, and myth, accompanied by more than 300 rare illustrations of planets, the Milky Way, signs of the zodiac, comets, meteors, and other astronomical phenomena. 192pp. 8⅜ x 11. 0-486-43981-X

JEWELRY MAKING: Techniques for Metal, Tim McCreight. Easy-to-follow instructions and carefully executed illustrations describe tools and techniques, use of gems and enamels, wire inlay, casting, and other topics. 72 line illustrations and diagrams. 176pp. 8¼ x 10⅞. 0-486-44043-5

MAKING BIRDHOUSES: Easy and Advanced Projects, Gladstone Califf. Easy-to-follow instructions include diagrams for everything from a one-room house for bluebirds to a forty-two-room structure for purple martins. 56 plates; 4 figures. 80pp. 8¾ x 6⅜. 0-486-44183-0

LITTLE BOOK OF LOG CABINS: How to Build and Furnish Them, William S. Wicks. Handy how-to manual, with instructions and illustrations for building cabins in the Adirondack style, fireplaces, stairways, furniture, beamed ceilings, and more. 102 line drawings. 96pp. 8¾ x 6⅜. 0-486-44259-4

THE SEASONS OF AMERICA PAST, Eric Sloane. From "sugaring time" and strawberry picking to Indian summer and fall harvest, a whole year's activities described in charming prose and enhanced with 79 of the author's own illustrations. 160pp. 8¼ x 11. 0-486-44220-9

THE METROPOLIS OF TOMORROW, Hugh Ferriss. Generous, prophetic vision of the metropolis of the future, as perceived in 1929. Powerful illustrations of towering structures, wide avenues, and rooftop parks–all features in many of today's modern cities. 59 illustrations. 144pp. 8¼ x 11. 0-486-43727-2

THE PATH TO ROME, Hilaire Belloc. This 1902 memoir abounds in lively vignettes from a vanished time, recounting a pilgrimage on foot across the Alps and Apennines in order to "see all Europe which the Christian Faith has saved." 77 of the author's original line drawings complement his sparkling prose. 272pp. 5⅜ x 8½. 0-486-44001-X

THE HISTORY OF RASSELAS: Prince of Abissinia, Samuel Johnson. Distinguished English writer attacks eighteenth-century optimism and man's unrealistic estimates of what life has to offer. 112pp. 5⅜ x 8½. 0-486-44094-X

A VOYAGE TO ARCTURUS, David Lindsay. A brilliant flight of pure fancy, where wild creatures crowd the fantastic landscape and demented torturers dominate victims with their bizarre mental powers. 272pp. 5⅜ x 8½. 0-486-44198-9

Paperbound unless otherwise indicated. Available at your book dealer, online at **www.doverpublications.com**, or by writing to Dept. GI, Dover Publications, Inc., 31 East 2nd Street, Mineola, NY 11501. For current price information or for free catalogs (please indicate field of interest), write to Dover Publications or log on to **www.doverpublications.com** and see every Dover book in print. Dover publishes more than 500 books each year on science, elementary and advanced mathematics, biology, music, art, literary history, social sciences, and other areas.